GYMKHANA!

Lesley Eccles
and
Linda Burgess

G·Y·M·K·H·A·N·A

David & Charles
Newton Abbot London
North Pomfret (Vt)

CONTENTS

Line illustrations by Joy Claxton

British Library Cataloguing in Publication Data

Eccles, Lesley
  Gymkhana!
   1. Gymkhanas (Horsemanship)
   I. Title   II. Burgess, Linda
   798.2'4   SF296.G9

   ISBN 0-7153-9122-4

Typeset by Typesetters (Birmingham) Limited,
Smethwick, West Midlands
and printed in Great Britain
by Redwood Burn Limited, Trowbridge, Wilts
for David & Charles Publishers plc
Brunel House Newton Abbot Devon

Published in the United States of America
by David & Charles Inc
North Pomfret Vermont 05053 USA

1
GYMKHANA!

It's Saturday evening at the Horse of the Year Show in October – the final night of one of Britain's most popular and prestigious celebrations of the horse. The last performance at Wembley Arena is known for the exciting, top-class showjumping; for the majesty of the heavy horses; for the thrill of seeing the beauty and elegance of the country's top show animals and for the emotional cavalcade, with its moving tribute to the horse, that brings the evening to a close.

Amongst all the quality horses, rubbing shoulders with the expensive showjumpers, superb hunters and impeccably trained police horses are the gymkhana ponies. They're the flying stars of the week, snatching their moments of glory – for whenever these ordinary ponies appear they have an extraordinary effect. They are guaranteed to almost raise the roof as the audience erupts with cheers of encouragement and animated applause.

The Prince Philip Cup is their competition – and Saturday evening's performance is the highlight of the week for the Pony Club teams that vie for the coveted honour of holding this splendid trophy aloft as they gallop a lap of honour and proclaim themselves Mounted Games' Champions.

Months of hard work and fierce competition are brought to a head; during Horse of the Year Show week children and ponies have made regular appearances to contest a variety of races. There have been laughter and tears and of the six teams to reach Wembley only the leading four will sweep through the famous arena entrance on the Saturday evening.

By Saturday the pressure is really on – there are double points to be gained. As the red curtain is thrown aside all eyes focus on the colourful riders and teams taking centre stage.

For the next few minutes Wembley explodes with excitement – relatives, friends and supporters of the teams line the hallowed arena, cheering, groaning, inspiring, consoling – the atmosphere is electric and no-one can stay still or fail to become involved.

The audience, encouraged by the commentator, call out for the various teams, becoming as engrossed as the young riders in this superb display of team work and riding skill. Ponies and riders take on the appearance of mini whirlwinds – how on earth will they stop once they've crossed the finishing line? But stop they do – demonstrating amazing ability, agility and timing.

Some games are carried out at tremendous speed – yet the saddles have been stripped off the ponies – bareback or not, it seems to make little difference to the confident, bold youngsters who are truly part of their ponies.

Thunderous applause echoes around as the final race is won – one team has made this year's Wembley theirs and theirs alone and it's their Pony Club branch that will be added to the roll of honour. For the individual children there are the rosettes, the wonderful memories of being part of the Horse of the Year Show and the knowledge that they are *The Champions*!

Children of all ages and abilities can enjoy themselves

Countless other youngsters watch the Prince Philip Cup on television, dreaming of being part of that special week, even though their current involvement in mounted games is a far cry from Wembley. For throughout the summer thousands of children all over Britain compete in mounted games. The fact that the venue is the tiny village fund-raising gymkhana is not important – for these youngsters and spectators the competition is just as nerve-wracking.

Of all the riders who compete in gymkhanas, some will join the Pony Club and go on to contest a place in their branch team; others, Pony Club members or not, will continue to compete happily at local level – and if that's you there's some help to improve your performance later.

For some riders the attraction of mounted games is such that they do not wish to give up once they've passed the Pony Club age limit (for mounted games only) of 15. This is where the Mounted Games Association of Great Britain plays a valuable part in encouraging competition and friendship through mounted games for riders up to the age of 21.

A rider's fascination with games on horseback is not a new phenomenon – throughout history 'games' have been used by all kinds of horsemen to demonstrate their skills or to entertain others.

In the thirteenth century mounted entertainments were provided by jousting tournaments – fields were specially prepared as the jousting arena and the events were held for fun as well as for more serious purposes, ie training for war.

British Army personnel in the mid- to late-nineteenth century used mounted games as a way of improving their skills, keeping fit and adding interest to life. Our word gymkhana dates from the days of the Army in India – gymkhana means a 'field day on horseback'.

Polo was one of the games played by Britishers stationed in India – but it is a sport dating from much earlier days: it's believed that a form of polo was played by the Persians as long ago as 500BC.

In the United States of America the skills required by cowboys, mounted on their nimble cutting or quarter horses, are also incorporated into entertaining displays.

However, mounted games in the form we think of them in Britain, have spread across the world – through the British Pony Club with its connections to clubs in numerous countries, eg Saudi Arabia, Kenya and Thailand, and through the MGAGB, which does a great deal to promote international competition with European championships as well as a trophy contested by teams from Canada, the USA and the United Kingdom.

The Pony Club's Mounted Games Championships

The first Pony Club Mounted Games Championship for the Prince Philip Cup took place in 1957 at the Horse of the Year Show following a successful pilot scheme inspired by HRH Prince Philip, Duke of Edinburgh, and organised by Col Sir Michael Ansell, then Director of the London Horse Shows and the HOYS.

A man always keen to promote new activities in the equestrian world, Col Sir Michael Ansell decided to give the proposed games a trial run by arranging for teams from north west Kent to take part in

All smiles from members of the Eglington Pony Club – one of the more well known names in the Prince Philip Cup's history (Basil Birchall)

mounted games. The event was an immediate success.

His next move was to approach HRH Prince Philip with the idea of including the games at the Horse of the Year Show. The suggestion was met with wholehearted approval from the Duke, who pledged a trophy to be presented annually to the winning team at the Horse of the Year Show.

It was felt that the competition should be geared towards children with ordinary ponies and the objectives of the games are to teach children discipline, good horsemanship and team spirit in an atmosphere of fun.

Having decided on the games' format and their introduction, there was one outstanding 'item' to be dealt with – that of finding a suitable sponsor. This came in the form of Butlin's, the holiday company, which provided financial support for fifteen years before withdrawing from the HOYS in 1982; then the financial responsibility of the competition was taken over by Dalgety Spillers, the equine feed specialists, and the Daily Mail Newspaper Group.

One of the best known and most loved characters connected with the Prince Philip Cup Mounted Games is Raymond Brooks-Ward who has been involved since the early days. This man shoulders the responsibility for the games at the HOYS and it is something he clearly enjoys. Throughout the week Raymond Brooks-Ward delivers a running commentary, whips up support from the audience for the teams and captures all the enthusiasm and thrills associated with mounted games. Indeed, the games are now known affectionately as 'Uncle Raymond's mounted games'.

'It is a marvellous competition for the children' said Mr Brooks-Ward, 'for it teaches them discipline and competitiveness, but above all, and most importantly, it allows them to have fun. Imagine what it means to those children to get to the Horse of the Year Show for a week. It's a once-in-a-lifetime opportunity for them – and as long as we have a sponsor to carry on this great tradition of the Horse of the Year Show, there will always be the Prince Philip Cup Mounted Games Competition.'

However, there would be no annual competition without the Pony Club which is the governing body for the games. The Pony Club lays down the rules and decides upon which games to include for the various levels of the competition.

The Pony Club was founded in 1929 and is represented in twenty-five countries with a membership in the region of 100,000. Its aim is to 'encourage young people to ride and to learn to enjoy all kinds of sport connected with horses and riding. To provide instruction in riding and horsemastership and to instil in members the proper care of their animals. To promote the highest ideals of sportsmanship, citizenship and loyalty, thereby cultivating strength of character and self-discipline.'

There are more than 300 branches of the Pony Club in Britain alone. Often the branches are attached to a hunt and so may take their name from the local hunt. The branches are self-supporting, self-governing and self-contained but are administered by a district commissioner who carries out numerous duties on a voluntary basis, backed by a hard-working committee.

Every branch of the Pony Club has an equal opportunity to enter teams for the Prince Philip Cup, provided the members are eligible. The youngsters need to be active members of the branch, having attended at least three working rallies since July 1 of the previous year. Potential team candidates must also have been Pony Club

Whatever the level of competition, there's always enthusiastic support for the mounted games competitors

members for a year and be under 15 years of age on May 1 of the competitive year.

NB: working rallies are usually organised by the district commissioners during school holidays. They are intended to be fun, whilst providing adequate instruction in equitation, pony management, care of tack and other aspects of pony ownership.

There are three stages to the mounted games competitions: area meetings, zone finals and then the ultimate venue, the Horse of the Year Show for the final of the competition.

At each stage the competition is run on a points system, with the winners of a race scoring a number of points equivalent to the number of teams competing that day, eg six points for a win if six teams are taking part. The second-placed team scores one point less and so on, with the team that comes last scoring just one point. In the case of equal placings the points are divided.

The first round of the competition, ie the area events, is usually held during the Easter holidays. There are nineteen area qualifying events in all, including contenders from Northern Ireland. This stage of the contest attracts between two and three hundred teams so competition is indeed fierce.

Branches attend their own area meeting, with the venue decided by the Pony Club. Six games are used, and the teams vie with one another for a place in the next stage of the contest, the zone finals.

Like the area meetings, the locations of the zone finals are decided by the Pony Club. Six zone finals are held during the school summer holidays with teams competing in ten events. Each zone produces a winning team, which has the honour of appearing at Wembley.

Those youngsters lucky enough to get through the well-disciplined but fun-filled zone finals spend the whole week at the Horse of the Year Show, competing in various events on championship nights, which usually run midweek from Wednesday to Saturday.

In addition to the games performances there's a healthy rivalry at the stable block where each team decorates its own stables whilst maintaining the highest standards of management. Walking around the Pony Club stables at this superb show is great fun, with some superb and amusing stable nameplates being provided by the teams.

Along the route to Wembley the children really have to earn their places – and the hard work certainly does not stop there. Nothing is won until the finishing line has been crossed and Lady Luck plays

A lap of honour for the Eglington as they win a zone final so earning them a place at the 1987 Horse of the Year Show (Basil Birchall)

only a small part in the success of teams, as Peter Lord, Chairman of the Pony Club Mounted Games, pointed out:

'It is basically down to the ability of the children and the training of the ponies. It is really quite extraordinary how the expertise has developed to the standard it is today.

'The format of the games has not changed over the past twenty-plus years but the standard has. It is indeed extremely high and is improving all the time.'

Mr Lord does not see the games changing at all – but he does predict that they will become even more professional.

Mounted Games Association of Great Britain

If teams from the MGAGB are entertaining the crowds at your county show, you'll know when it's time for the mounted games. For the MGAGB teams are introduced by the famous and stirring music of *The Magnificent Seven.* It's an apt choice as the association was founded in 1984 by seven geographical entities – six counties – Avon, Berkshire, Hampshire, Hertfordshire, Surrey, Sussex – and south west Wales. Such is the appeal of mounted games that at the time of writing there are forty-four member counties.

The association's object is 'to encourage friendship between young people of different nations' and this is developing well, as there are now teams from Belgium, the Netherlands, Italy, Canada, USA, Southern Ireland and Sweden as well as from England, Wales, Scotland and Northern Ireland.

Although it is separate from the Pony Club and is not affiliated to the British Horse Society, there are still strong links between the MGAGB and the Pony Club. The Mounted Games Association developed from the Pony Club but whereas the PC is hunt-based the MGAGB concentrates on counties. In some cases, officials involved in training Pony Club teams also participate in the MGAGB.

John Bycroft, from Lincolnshire, is the county representative, as well as being chairman of the northern committee. John, his wife and three children had ten very successful years with the Burghley branch of the Pony Club before continuing their connection with mounted games via the MGAGB.

'The association gave our children the opportunity to continue on the ponies they had trained over the years. They enjoyed mounted games because of the team spirit and fun,' explained John.

'Norman Patrick, who used to be chairman of the Pony Club Mounted Games Committee, started the MGA three years ago,' he added, 'the upper age limit for our riders is twenty-one and we now get lots of youngsters trying for places in our team. At one time it was mainly youngsters who had outgrown the Pony Club games, but we're now being seen more at shows and the appeal has widened.

'As far as the riders are concerned, because it is a team event everyone is dependent upon everyone else to do his bit. They have to work for each other and operate as a team. When the riders are in the ring they are there to win but as soon as the competition is over all the riders are friends.'

With the increasing popularity of the games, some counties are able to field two teams. Lincolnshire, for instance, at the time of writing has about ten riders from which to select a team. Some of these riders live sixty miles away from others, so practice sessions are not always easy to arrange.

John explained that it is not always the fastest riders who make the team. 'Look for a team that is consistent – it is not always made up of the fastest riders because the faster you go the more likely you are to make mistakes. Team members have to know the maximum limit they can work to. Fast riders are okay but you may win three races and be last in three, and because everything works on a points system you could be well down the final placings.

'We work on a team that does not make many mistakes – members are the ones who will be there or thereabouts at the end of the competition. We try to tell riders not to take chances, to go for the points not necessarily for the win.

'From the trainer's point of view, the satisfaction is not purely in the team winning a competition. Whether the team wins or is last, if the trainer has prepared the riders to the best of his or her ability and the riders are trained to the best of their ability; if they have enjoyed the show, tried their best but finished last, what more can you ask?'

Enjoyment and friendship constitute the game for the MGAGB teams – and for spectators at shows where the county teams entertain, there's the added pleasure of being able to actively support their own county representatives.

'Riders are not paid to appear at the venues and the MGAGB simply asks for a donation towards their overheads. The riders appear for pleasure and the venue gains because there's something to fill the showring and provide fun and entertainment for the spectators,' said John.

In fact the MGAGB displays are proving so popular and the association is growing at such a rate that there's increased competition for places in teams and there are more teams willing and able to give displays. More venues are needed for the colourful teams who sport special colours bearing the emblem of the association and the name of their county or region.

The MGAGB has a number of trophies that are contested regularly:

- The Mike Ansell Cup for the Home International Championship, presented by the association's patron, Col Sir Michael Ansell, CBE, DSO, DL.
- The Duke of Wellington Cup for the European Championship presented by His Grace The Duke of Wellington, MVO, OBE, MC, DL.
- The Douro Cup for the first team from the continent of Europe presented by The Marquess of Douro, MEP.
- The Churchill Cup for the Championship between Canada, USA and UK presented by Winston Churchill, Esq, MP.
- The President's Cup for the Inter-Counties Championship presented by the association's president, Richard Simmonds, Esq, MEP.
- The Chairman's Cup for the trainer of the Inter-Counties Championship winners, presented by Lt Col Donald Clark, the association's founder chairman.
- The Runwick Cup for the highest placed team after the preliminary rounds of the Inter-Counties Championship presented by MGAGB Director, Norman Patrick.
- A Challenge Cup for the trainer of the Runwick Cup winner, presented by John Bullock, Esq.

2
THE GYMKHANA
PONY AND RIDER

Mix together a forward-going pony, a confident rider, lots of practice, time, luck and commitment and you're on the way to a successful mounted games partnership.

Spectators often marvel at the speed and skill of mounted games competitors without realising the huge amount of work that goes on 'behind the scenes' to produce a slick pony and rider combination. Good games' riders are those who view competitions as the chance to put all their homework to the test. Unsuccessful competitors are those who take their ponies to shows to 'learn the ropes' without taking the trouble to practise anything or learn new skills at home first.

Whether success at the local gymkhana or a place in your county mounted games team is your aim, the basic requirements for both pony and rider are the same.

Virtually any pony can be trained for mounted games as John Bycroft, Lincolnshire county representative of the Mounted Games Association of Great Britain, explained:

'You can start with any kind of pony so long as it is a forward-going animal, not something which naps, goes backward or up in the air. If the pony is a forward-going type then he can be schooled quite easily.

'I've found that the best ponies are the unspoilt ones. If you buy one that has done a few gymkhanas and has been pulled around or allowed to get into bad habits, then it can be quite a job to get the pony right. If a pony doesn't know anything then you can train it to do exactly what you want and make it into a good pony.'

One important criterion for a good games pony is size. You may think that a 14.2hh would be great as, being bigger, it can cover the ground faster than a smaller pony. Yet when it comes to weaving in and out of bending poles and turning on a sixpence the larger pony is at a disadvantage. Therefore the more serious gymkhana competitors look to smaller ponies eg, 12.2hh to 13hh for riders up to about

---

Your pony says RELAX!
Everyone gets nervous in competitions but try to overcome your nerves and relax – if you're too tense your pony will feel it, become over-excited and will not be able to give of his best.

An ordinary child's pony . . . with time and practice most ponies can become competent gymkhana contenders

fourteen years of age and 13.2hh to 13.3hh for older teenagers. Even in the MGAGB, where riders can compete up to the age of twenty-one and may be 5ft 8in tall, ponies around 13.3hh are used.

Smaller ponies have another advantage; they are much easier for young riders to vault on to!

As this is a fast sport, contestants need to be bold, confident riders who possess the will to win. Competition, particularly further up the ladder of Pony Club and the MGAGB, is tough. A good gymkhana rider also needs to be fairly athletic to cope with the demands of running, vaulting on and off and leaning down as the pony moves at great speed.

It's also vital that a rider keeps a cool head despite all the excitement and activity around him or her. Mistakes do happen and the rider has to be able to correct them quickly, forget them and get on with the job of crossing the finishing line. There's no place for the rider who gets upset or gives up in the middle of a heat – particularly

A pony who will stay calm and obedient whatever his rider is doing is needed

if it is a team event. However, before any combination can reach the dizzy heights of competition there's plenty of work to be done at home.

Training

In addition to being forward-going, a good games pony needs to be obedient and balanced. His job requires him to gallop from a standstill, turn quickly, stand quietly whilst the rider performs various tasks and much more. The gymkhana pony will be racing against other ponies and, if he is a part of a team, may find other ponies hurtling towards him.

A pony can take all this in his stride, providing he is trained properly. His education will include general schooling, which all horses and ponies undergo, plus some specific gymkhana preparation.

General schooling: there are many relatively simple exercises that can be incorporated into a pony's work programme to improve his way of going. Young riders are often less than enthusiastic about flatwork, yet there's no need for schooling to be boring for either pony or rider.

Work may be carried out in a special area set aside for the purpose (perhaps in a corner of the field) or as the pony is being ridden out on hacks.

If you wish to mark out an arena, choose the levellest part of your field and try to aim for an area about 130ft by 65ft (40m by 20m). Cones, large upturned cans or boxes can be used to mark the four corners of the arena. A set of dressage markers will add a professional touch to your outdoor 'school'. These are relatively inexpensive to buy or you can make a set using large old paint cans, buckets or wooden markers on to which the letters A, C, B, E, K, F, H and M have been painted. Arrange the letters as shown in Fig 1.

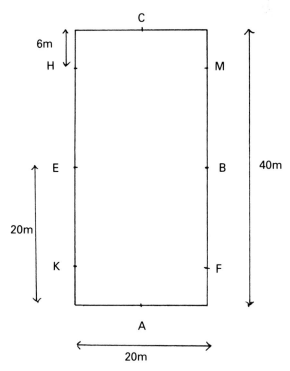

Fig 1 Dimensions for a working arena with the universal lettering system

It's important that a pony's work is varied and interesting for him; this logic should also apply when you are planning a schooling session. A variety of school movements is featured later but before you launch yourself into flatwork there are a few points to consider:

a) Always have a warming up period before you do any serious work with your pony. If you think about it, athletes undertake some loosening up exercises before they hurdle, attempt the high jump and so on. Your pony also needs a warm up period so that his muscles can be loosened and his body and mind prepared for the work ahead.

This period can be of ten to fifteen minutes' duration when you will ask the pony to walk and trot on both reins. Concentrate on getting the pony moving forwards actively and obediently. Use rising trot as this is easier on the pony's back, then finish off the warming up time with a short canter on each rein.

b) Have an idea of which exercises you wish to cover in your session and for how long you intend to work. You should think and prepare ahead to give your pony the best chance of obeying you and producing a better performance.

c) Remember to work on both reins to prevent your pony becoming one-sided. It's usual for horses and ponies to have a stiff side, although the degree of the problem can vary from animal to animal. You may need to work your pony a little more on his stiffer side.

d) It is worth having regular riding lessons, even if you have been riding and competing for some time. An instructor on the ground will be able to identify any problems and advise you on ways of dealing with difficulties.

e) If you are an inexperienced pony owner, instruction is particularly valuable to keep you on the right track.

f) Always finish a work session on a good note – this helps to keep the mental approach of both pony and rider on a healthier footing.

g) Each session should end with a cooling down period to relax your pony and let him dry if he's been sweating. Walk your pony around the field for a little while or go for a short hack.

h) Vary your schooling, eg by using hacks out as an opportunity to practise transitions, etc.

i) Do not make flatwork sessions too long – two or three twenty-minute periods a week are better than one marathon work period.

School movements and terms
When you are working your pony you are aiming to achieve free relaxed forward-movement, good rhythm and suppleness. If you reach these goals your pony will be balanced and therefore better able to compete in the fast moving world of mounted games.

To move forward freely a pony needs to be paying attention to his rider so that when the lightest of aids is given the pony responds willingly and energetically. When you are working in your pony before a schooling session, frequent transitions are a good way of waking him up and gaining his attention. Half-halts are also used as a way of telling the pony to pay attention.

Every time you ride try to be aware of the rhythm of your pony's movement. In walk there are four beats to every stride and there should be a regularity and evenness to each hoofbeat. Watch how a

---

Routine checks
* Whenever you pick out your pony's feet check that his shoes are okay – remember the signs which indicate a visit from the farrier is needed, ie loose shoes; overgrown toes; risen clenches; thin shoes; an overlong and out of shape foot.
* If your pony's in good health he'll be bright, alert and acting normally. If anything is amiss you should be able to notice this by changes in his behaviour and appearance eg he may appear dull and listless; his coat could 'stare' rather than bloom; he may be sweating, restless and generally appear uncomfortable; he may not have eaten up his feed/hay; perhaps the number of droppings passed overnight has decreased – if you notice anything out of the ordinary check for other signs that the pony is 'off colour'.
* Normal temperature for a pony is 100 to 101°F.
* At rest a pony's normal pulse beat will be between 36–42 beats per minute.
* Usual respiration rate is 8–15 per minute.
* To ensure your pony is in tip-top health you need to know what is normal for him (remember that every animal is an individual – so check you pony's temperature, pulse etc now). You must learn to observe and take action if anything is not quite normal.
* Keeping a pony in good condition relies on good feeding, proper stable management, appropriate exercise and paying attention to detail.

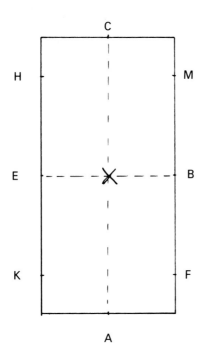

Fig 2 In lessons or dressage tests you'll hear the 'centre line' referred to. This is an imaginary line from C to A. Where it intersects with an imaginary line from E-B is the spot X. This is not marked on any arena

pony's legs move in walk, trot and canter – then try to feel what is happening when you ride at these paces.

Walk is a four-time pace with the legs moving in the following sequence:

1 Near-hind
2 Near-fore
3 Off-hind
4 Off-fore

The trot is a two-time pace, as the pony moves his legs in diagonal pairs with a period of suspension as he springs from one diagonal to the other. A pony's off-fore and near-hind move together as the right diagonal, while the near-fore and off-hind are the left diagonal.

Canter is a three-time pace. Working on the right rein the sequence of the pony's legs would be:

1 Near-hind
2 Off-hind and near-fore together
3 Off-fore

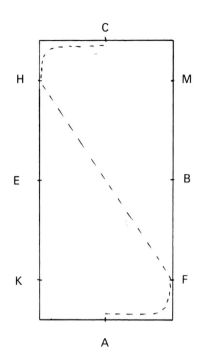

C

H   M

E   B

K   F

A

Fig 3 A change of rein across the diagonal. The diagonal M-K may also be used. Changes of rein are needed frequently to ensure that a pony does not become one-sided

There's a moment of suspension before the sequence starts again. In this example the off-fore is the leading leg as the pony is cantering on the right rein. On the left rein the near-fore is the leading leg.

Count out the rhythm of each pace as you ride along – this will help increase your familiarity and feel for your pony's paces.

The third ingredient that helps to make a balanced pony is suppleness, both laterally (ie, side to side) and longitudinally (ie, from the pony's head to tail, along the length of his body). There are a host of exercises that can help to create suppleness but, to achieve the required response from the pony, the rider needs to be sitting properly and applying the aids correctly.

Check out your position with this list: sit in the deepest part of the saddle with your weight evenly divided between your two seat bones; sit tall but not stiffly; make sure you are sitting square and level; look where you are going; let your arms hang naturally so that your elbows are touching your sides and there is a straight line through your lower arms along the reins to the pony's mouth; your lower legs should be lightly touching the pony's side (with your stirrup leather hanging vertical to the ground); as your weight is

31

Just look at them go! Riders competing in a Pony Club Home International at the Royal Windsor Horse Show (Horse & Pony Magazine)

carried down through your legs and feet so your heels will drop slightly so that they are below the level of your toes; keep the stirrup iron on the ball of your foot, taking care not to point your toes inwards or outwards.

You should feel comfortable and natural. If you have to force yourself into a particular position you will simply be creating tension and riders cannot give of their best unless they are relaxed and tension free.

Whenever you ask a pony to move off, increase pace and so on, your instructions need to be crystal clear and applied correctly. You can use your seat, weight, legs, hands and voice to signal your intentions to a pony but you must remember that all these aids work in conjunction with each other. For example, there's more to stopping your pony than hauling on the reins! Before you apply any aids to halt, you should think and prepare. Your body and hands would stop following the movement of the pony in walk, while the legs would still be closed on the pony's sides to ensure that the pony brings his quarters under him for a square halt with his weight evenly distributed.

A rider's weight aids can be used to tremendous effect in mounted games. By shifting your weight onto one seat bone you are asking the pony to turn towards that side. As the rider has changed his centre of gravity so the pony moves towards the rider's new centre of gravity in order to balance himself. By subtle use of weight aids a rider can ask the pony to turn or circle, but the rider has to be careful not to collapse his body to one side.

Variety is the key to keeping both pony and rider interested during schooling sessions – combine transitions, changes of direction, circles, figures of eight, loops and serpentines.

Transitions: these are changes in pace and may be progressive, eg walk-trot-canter or acute, eg halt-trot. Aim for smooth transitions, with the pony moving forwards into the next pace. Even if the transition is a downward one, eg canter to trot, think of the forward movement into the next pace rather than letting the pony 'fall' into the transition and so losing activity.

Keep the rhythm of each pace until you change into the next pace – often you see ponies asked to canter and they run on, leaning on their forehands instead of smartly making the transition.

Work on progressive transitions first. If your pony does not respond to your aids (and providing your instructions were clear and that the pony knows what is required) then back up your aids with a reminder from your whip.

Always prepare and think ahead – do not suddenly decide to stop at A when you're only half a stride away from the marker.

Changes of rein and circles: young ponies that have received very little schooling will need to work in larger areas, on bigger circles and with more room to turn. As a pony becomes more supple and better trained so he can be worked on more demanding, smaller circles.

It's very easy when riding turns or circles to achieve too much bend in a pony's head and neck (these are two of the most pliant parts of a pony's body) while the rest of the body remains straight instead of curving around the track of the movement.

You should only be able to see the inside corner of the pony's eye as you're describing a circle. Think of riding inside leg to outside hand with the inside rein maintaining a slight flexion and the outside

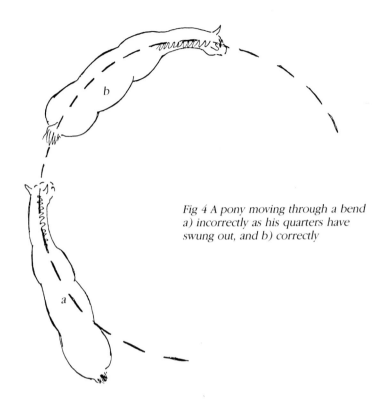

Fig 4 A pony moving through a bend
a) incorrectly as his quarters have
swung out, and b) correctly

leg ensuring that the pony's quarters do not swing out.

Twenty metre circles can be combined to form figures of eight; changes of rein can be carried out inside a 20m circle; two half 20m circles can be used to change the rein; you can spiral in and out of 20m circles; use 15 and 10m circles later to help a pony's suppleness.

Turn on the forehand: with this exercise the pony moves away from the rider's leg so that the pony's hind legs describe a circle around his front legs. For instance, on a right turn on the forehand the pony's right hind leg will cross over in front of the left hind leg, while the right front leg acts as a pivot being picked up and put down again in the same spot several times during the exercise.

The pony's body is slightly bent in the direction of the turn and he must not be allowed to step back during the movement. Once the exercise is completed the pony should be moved forwards promptly.

If a pony can execute this turn it makes life much easier, for example when you have to open and close a gate out hacking.

Gymkhana training

During gymkhana games, ponies have to cope with all kinds of situations that they would not normally meet in the course of their daily work – for example, their riders hopping alongside them in sacks, squeezy bottles being grabbed off poles, riders running alongside and vaulting on as the pony canters along, even straw filled 'bodies' being flung across their withers.

A pony, therefore, needs to be accustomed to all kinds of sights and sounds before he even enters the gymkhana ring. He needs to be as unflappable as possible. This is where regular practice at home is required – start off at walk, introducing the pony to coloured barrels, waving flags, sacks on the floor, brightly coloured objects and so on. If the pony has confidence in his rider and is kindly, but firmly shown that there's nothing to fear from sudden, strange noises or a huge variety of objects, progress will be much quicker.

This competitor would find life easier if she could teach her pony to lead alongside . . . it would help her as she runs along the stepping stones

THE GYMKHANA PONY AND RIDER

Once the pony is happy working among gymkhana props in all paces, then start to teach him to neck rein. It's a vital skill for riders to be able to control their ponies using just one hand on the reins, thus freeing the other hand for holding flags, etc.

Here's how John Bycroft from the Lincolnshire branch of the MGAGB helps his young riders to master the art: 'Start off in walk with the reins knotted, holding the knot in the palm of the hand. The basic movements of the rider's hands are forwards, back, right and left but the rider has to think about weight aids. I always tell the youngsters to think of riding a bicycle – they would lean with the bike around a turn or they'd fall off. If they use their weight properly the pony will follow it and turn, for example, when going through bending poles.

'They start off at walk, using their legs for turning the pony and making use of their seats – it's surprising how many riders you see who just sit on their ponies without using the seat as an aid. Most riders soon take to using just one hand for control. At first some of them worry about stopping the pony, or being able to turn, but a pony has to slow down for a turn. If the pony tried to turn at a gallop without slowing first then he'd fall over.'

With these skills mastered it's time for the rider to acquire the technique of leaning well down to pick up flags, place potatoes in buckets and so on. The rider needs to be agile and confident while the pony has to be quite happy about all this activity, accepting it without napping or altering speed.

Accuracy is an important attribute – if you miss a flag you'll only waste time in going back. For instance, if you need to drop something into a container on the ground the closer you can get to it, the more chance you have of placing the object in the container rather than throwing it in and hoping that the object will reach its target successfully.

Start by leaning down on either side of your pony at walk, then trot and make sure you feel happy about it and are secure before trying this technique at canter and gallop.

Many gymkhana games call for the rider to remove or replace items, eg the flag race. A better chance of success is offered if the

Reaching forward for a cup . . . you'll have a better chance of securing the object if you attack it in this way

rider has arm and hand extended to the front rather than to the side. Then, by leaning forward slightly too, the rider can be on top of what is to be grabbed. As you are travelling forwards at quite a fast rate it makes sense to stretch out and take something in front of you; if you do miss, you have a second chance as you pass by the flag.

Lots of practice is needed – after all the top of each container holding flags is only about three inches (7.5cm) across and that looks even smaller when seen from the top of a pony!

Trying various games at home will also give you the chance to experiment with different techniques to overcome problems. For instance, in the stepping stones race it's easy to kick one of the stones out unless you move them properly. By running over the stones 'flat-footed' you ensure that all the props stay in place.

If you can ensure that you're accurate when dealing with whatever actually makes up the game, then you can make up speed on the flat in between the obstacles. It's no use being the fastest partnership if you then waste time by missing flags, having to circle because you've broken into a canter during the trotting race, missed a bending pole or whatever. Accuracy and consistency are the goals to aim for.

Get together with some friends for your practice sessions to give all the ponies the opportunity to race against each other before they get into the ring. Games do excite ponies and if animals become too 'hot' they can be difficult to manage. Try to introduce all elements of games to your pony gradually so that they become part of life and he does not become unduly difficult or excitable.

If you do your homework before you even enter a show you're giving your pony the best chance of starting his gymkhana career with a bang! As John Bycroft explained, 'When my children first started we used to practise four or five times a week, getting the ponies used to anything and everything. With fairly experienced riders, who do not let ponies become naughty, it's possible to take a green pony and have him up to a decent standard within about six weeks.'

Part of your practice sessions can include riding bareback and vaulting on – two essential skills for those wishing to make it to the top levels of mounted games. Riding bareback, in safe, supervised surroundings, will help to improve your seat, balance and confidence.

Both riders and ponies should enjoy mounted games – be careful

X = trotting pole   ☐ = jump

X◄— 4½ft —►**X**◄— 4½ft —►**X**

Fig 5a Set your trotting poles about 4½ feet apart – distances do vary according to the pony's/horse's stride, but 4½ feet is generally suitable unless the pony is tiny. Trot through the poles, aiming for the centre

X◄—4½ft—►**X**◄—4½ft—►**X**◄——— 9ft ———►☐

b Once the pony is happy with trotting poles, a small jump can be placed 9 feet away from the final pole. Working through exercises such as this will help to make any pony more agile

X◄—4½ft—►**X**◄—4½ft—►**X**◄——— 9ft ———►☐◄——— 9ft ———►**X**

c If your pony rushes and becomes unbalanced, add another pole 9 feet after the jump in order to steady him

X◄—4½ft—►**X**◄—4½ft—►**X**◄——— 9ft ———►☐◄——— 9ft ———►**X**◄——— 9ft ———►☐

d Further jumps and poles can be added to make the grid more difficult. Remember to ride straight down the grid, keep your legs on and ride positively

not to overdo the practice. Let the partnerships relax and have a little variety in their work by hacking out, going through jumping grids, taking in crosscountry and showjumping classes at shows, etc.

Hacks can be used in a positive way to help the pony – eg, practise transitions and moving the pony away from your leg as you ride along quiet tracks, or use a corner of a common as a schooling area instead of your usual working area.

Working through gymnastic jumping grids sharpens up both the pony and rider. Exercises such as going through without reins or stirrups can also help your seat and balance.

Keep both pony and rider fresh and having fun.

3
SADDLERY

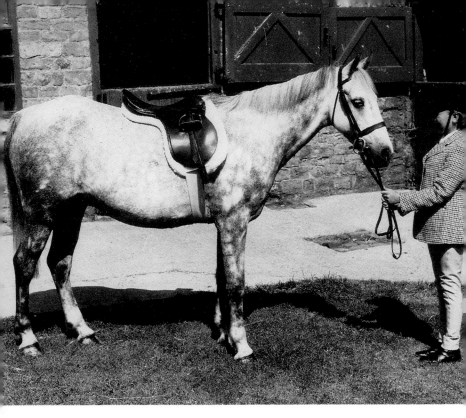

No special tack is required . . . but well fitting and well cared for equipment is essential

No special tack is required for mounted games but as with any saddlery it's essential that the equipment is suitable for the pony, fits well, is of good quality and properly cared for.

In the MGAGB, snaffle bits, either plain or twisted, metal or rubber are allowed provided, as John Bycroft says, 'It is not too severe or hurting the pony. A pony can be trained to do what you want without using contraptions. You must not be cruel to the pony.'

No bit is allowed to have any additional attachments to increase its severity. If a rider wishes to use a hackamore bitless bridle or a gag snaffle, a request, supported by a veterinary certificate, has to be submitted to the referee.

For the Pony Club the bit must be a plain snaffle with a straight bar or a single joint in the middle. The mouthpiece has to be smooth all round. Bitless bridles are not permitted. Martingales may be worn.

The Pony Club does not permit Kineton nosebands. Plaited nylon

---

Tack cleaning tip
Get rid of 'jockeys' – those little lumps of grease that gather on tack
– by using some of your pony's tail hair rolled into a ball.

---

reins are ideal as they are supple and can be knotted easily. A saddle
with a high cantle can present problems when the rider vaults on.

Ponies may wear protective boots, eg brushing/tendon boots and
studs can also be used in the pony's hind shoes for extra grip in
slippery conditions.

Fitting of tack

Tack must fit correctly or it can injure the pony. Regular checks are
advised to ensure that the saddle tree has not been broken and to
determine whether the saddle needs restuffing. All stitching and
buckles should also be inspected for safety reasons.

Saddles
It is important that a saddle distributes the rider's weight evenly on
the pony's back and without exerting any pressure on the pony's

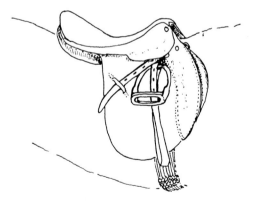

*Fig 6 Saddles must be fitted carefully to avoid pressure on the spine and
withers*

For young riders safety stirrups are sensible precautions. Leading rein classes are a good introduction to competition for the very young

spine. Saddles should not place any weight on the loins – the weakest part of a pony's back.

When the rider is mounted, there should be a clear channel between the pony's spine and the saddle gullet along the entire length of the saddle. If a numnah is used, make sure it is pulled well up into the gullet and front arch so that undue pressure is not brought to bear on the pony's spine.

It's also vital to ensure that the withers are not pressed upon or pinched. There needs to be adequate clearance by the saddle's front arch – you ought to be able to fit three fingers between the withers and arch.

As ponies vary in size so saddles come in different fittings – narrow, medium and wide– thus there's no excuse for the saddle pinching the withers. A pony just brought up from a holiday at grass will obviously be a different shape from a fit pony in work; it is therefore wise to check the fit of a saddle regularly.

Conformation (ie, the shape of the pony) faults may result in the saddle slipping either forwards or backwards. This can easily be rectified by the use of a crupper in the first case or a breastplate to

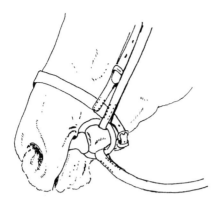

Fig 7 A correctly fitted cavesson noseband

help prevent the latter. At the least, a badly fitting saddle can hamper a pony's movement, but if saddle galls and injured backs result then a considerable period off work will follow.

Bridles
The browband is there simply to stop the bridle headpiece from slipping back, but you must ensure that the browband does not touch or pinch the pony's ears.

Throatlashes that are fitted too tightly restrict the pony's breathing and capability to flex. If fitted correctly, an adult should be able to place the full width of the hand between the throatlash and the side of the pony's jaw.

Cavesson nosebands are adjusted so that they lie halfway between the projecting cheek bone and the corners of the mouth. A simple check to ensure that it is fitted properly is to insert two fingers' breadth between the noseband and the front of the pony's face.

Drop nosebands need careful adjustment as otherwise they can hamper the pony's breathing. A common fault is to fit them too low so that they are tightened across the nostrils. At the front the drop

---

Did you know?
That you can make a long-headed pony look better by using a wide noseband on him rather than a thin one?

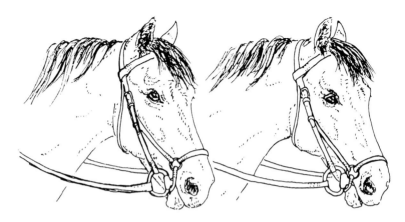

Fig 8 (left) Well fitting drop nosebands will not interfere with the horse's breathing. Fig 9 (right) This drop noseband is fitted too low, and will do more harm than good

noseband should lie well above the nostrils, while at the back it should fit into the chin groove.

Bits require careful selection and fitting. Ideally a pony should go kindly in a snaffle, but there are some ponies who need stronger bits in certain circumstances to ensure that the rider is in full control.

A bit needs to be the correct width for the pony's mouth – if it is too wide it will bruise the mouth as it moves from side to side, if too narrow, pinching will result. There needs to be about a quarter of an inch (6mm) 'play' at either side – an easy way to check is to gently pull the bit to one side so that the opposite bit ring is against the pony's mouth. There should be approximately half an inch (12mm) between the pony's mouth and the bit ring.

If a pony wants to evade the action of the bit, he can quite easily do so by throwing up his head. Martingales are artificial aids that help to lower a pony's head and stop this evasion, so giving the rider more control. In a perfect world, of course, there would be no need for

Tip
Check your tack regularly for fitting – and remember that new leather stretches so will need adjusting within the first few days of use.

*Fig 10 Bits should be fitted so that they just
wrinkle the corners of the pony's mouth*

such items of tack, as all ponies would be sufficiently well schooled
so that they worked happily on the bit, with a relaxed back and their
hindquarters or 'engine' engaged. In the real world, however, there
is a definite need for martingales to be used on some animals so
riders ought to know the fitting checkpoints.

If properly fitted, a martingale will not interfere with the pony's
way of going but as soon as anything untoward happens it should
come into effect.

*Fig 11 (left) A flash noseband, combining the cavesson (to which a standing
martingale can be attached) with the extra strap which is similar to a drop
noseband. Fig 12 (right) Grakle nosebands exert pressure on the nose where
the straps intersect*

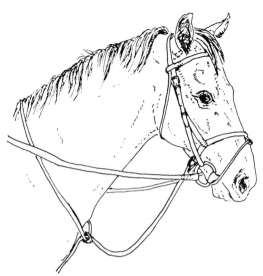

Fig 13 A standing martingale fitted with a flash noseband

Standing martingales are simple in their action. They consist of a leather strap with a loop at each end. One loop is attached to the pony's noseband and the other end passes between the pony's forelegs so that the girth can be slipped through it. If the martingale has cause to come into action, then force is exerted on the pony's nose. A standing martingale should be attached to a cavesson noseband; if you usually have a drop noseband on your pony, then

---

What and why?

A flash noseband is a cavesson noseband but with an extra strap sewn to the centre of the noseband which is fastened below the bit, rather like a drop noseband. This enables a standing martingale to be used (by attaching it to the cavesson part of the noseband) whilst the pony's mouth can be kept closed thanks to the extra strap. Sometimes ponies try to evade the action of the bit by opening their mouths and letting the bit slide through. A drop, flash or Grakle noseband will prevent this.

Grakle nosebands are also known as cross-over nosebands as the top straps fasten above the bit and the lower straps below the bit. Pressure is applied to the pony's nose at the point where the straps cross. It's a useful noseband for pullers or ponies who cross their jaws.

Fig 14 A running martingale correctly fitted so it only comes into action if the pony raises his head above the point of control

substitute a flash noseband, as standing martingales can be used in conjunction with these.

With the pony's head up in the correct position you ought to be able to bring up the front strap of the martingale so that it just reaches into the pony's gullet. Beware of fitting a standing martingale too tightly, or you'll restrict the pony's ability to stretch his neck.

A running martingale differs in that instead of one front strap it splits into two, with rings on each of the straps. The reins are then passed through these straps so that when the martingale comes into action there is pressure on the pony's mouth. This can be quite severe, especially if the martingale is fitted far too tightly. In order to prevent the rings of the martingale becoming looped onto the rein buckles where they attach to the bit, rubber stops are used on the reins between the martingale and bit.

When the martingale is attached to the girth, you should be able to take both front straps up one side of the pony's shoulder so that they reach the withers. If fitted too loosely, this martingale can be quite dangerous, as an excited pony could get caught up in the loops.

Both the standing and the running martingales have neckstraps to support them. These are fitted with the buckle on the nearside of the pony's neck and there should be room for the width of your hand to be admitted at the withers, ie about three inches (7.5cm).

Care of tack
Good quality saddlery is expensive but will last for years if properly treated. Time may prevent you from giving your pony's tack a thorough clean after every ride but you should always wash the bit after use. At least once a week dismantle your tack and clean it meticulously. Numnahs require particular attention as they can quickly become dirty and sweaty. Most types can now be washed easily in machines.

Tip
When you're cleaning your tack there's a quick and easy way to get rid of the gunge from the holes in your bridle and stirrup leathers. Simply use cocktail sticks!

Protective Boots

If you spend just a few extra minutes when tacking up you can shield your pony's legs against knocks and bruises.

Brushing boots are used to protect the inside of the legs near the fetlocks. There's a wide variety of boots made from various materials, such as leather and felt with leather or velcro fastenings. The boots are fitted so that the straps or fastenings point backwards and are on

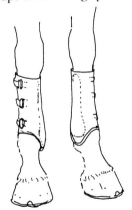

Fig 15 Brushing boots are a sensible precaution when working your pony

Protective boots may be required by some animals – it's certainly wise to wear them for practice sessions in order to protect your pony against knocks and bruises

the outside of the pony's legs. Longer brushing boots are needed on the hind legs than on the forelegs. To fit the boot, place it slightly above the area you wish to protect and then slide it into place so that the hair lies smooth. As you fasten the straps make sure the pressure is even all the way down the boot.

Your pony's legs should be clean and free of mud before the boots are fitted. Check there's no dirt on the inside of the boot that could also rub the pony's legs. As you remove the boots, rub the pony's legs to stimulate circulation.

Tendon boots protect and support the tendons. They are fitted in much the same way as brushing boots.

An over-reach wound can be quite a nasty injury so you may wish to safeguard your pony by using over-reach boots on his front feet.

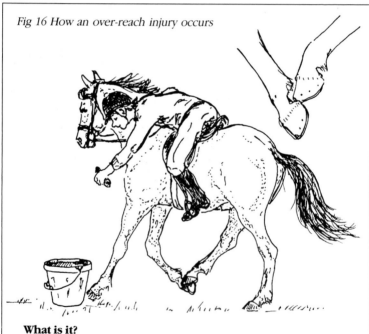

Fig 16 How an over-reach injury occurs

What is it?
An over-reach injury is caused by the toe of the pony's hind shoe catching the heel area of his front leg. This can happen because the pony has over-extended his hind legs eg when galloping. An over-reach injury can vary from a small bruise to a deep and nasty cut.

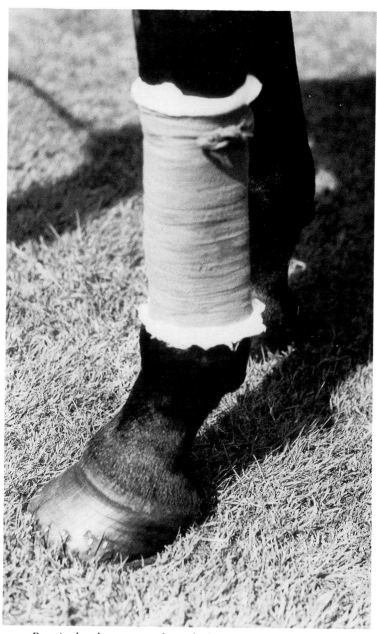

Exercise bandages, properly applied, are an alternative to boots

Exercise bandages are useful during fast work to protect and support the legs. However, it's essential they are fitted correctly. The bandages are made of elasticated material and they must be applied over gamgee or some other similar material. It's also vital that the pressure is even throughout and that the tapes are tied at the side of the leg, not on the bone at the front of the leg or the tendon at the back. Another sensible precaution is to apply sticky tape over the bandage ties so that the bandage cannot become undone during the pony's work.

Tip
Over-reach boots are a useful addition to your pony's travelling gear, especially if he tends to tread on himself in the trailer.

Studs

It's a rider's responsibility to ride any pony to the best of his or her ability, ensuring that the pony is balanced. However, there are times when a little help is needed to give a pony extra grip in slippery conditions. Studs in a pony's shoes can be the answer – it's rather a case of trial and error, as not all ponies like the feel of studs.

If you want to give studs a try, you'll have to ask your farrier to fit your pony's hind shoes with stud holes into which a variety of studs can be inserted. Consult your farrier for advice on the best type and size of stud for your purposes. Remember that if your pony does wear studs he'll be putting his feet down at an unnatural angle thus causing strain on the joints. Do not leave studs in for longer than necessary, especially if the pony is left to stand on a hard surface. Particular care should be taken if big studs are used – do not ride on roadways or hard surfaces. Big studs can also damage the floor of your trailer – as well as your foot if a pony treads on you!

4
PREPARING
YOUR PONY

Fitness

Training a pony for any competition requires proper care and attention. You cannot expect a pony that has been out at grass for most of the year to suddenly race around an arena, claiming all the prizes.

A special fitness programme needs to be worked out to fit in with your schedule of school work.

A pony that is out at grass, with little exercise, will undoubtedly develop a grass belly, which needs to be reduced considerably. Slow, gradual work will help to lose it.

Most gymkhana ponies are likely to be hardy animals that live out for much of the year, which works in well with their young riders who are at school. This is preferable as ponies generally keep healthier when living out.

The training programme given here is a general one designed for ponies that are kept out at grass. All ponies are individuals and you should work out a programme to suit both your own and your pony's needs.

If the animal has been rested for a while exercise should be conducted in small amounts, gradually building up to more intensive work. Start off by walking the pony out for half an hour a day for the first week, gradually building up to an hour. Make sure your pony walks out well, rather than slopping along. In the second week you can start to introduce short periods of trotting, gradually increasing the number and length of these over the next week to ten days. The length of your rides can also be gradually increased to an hour and a half by the third week.

Short canters can be worked into the programme by the fourth week and you can also incorporate some schooling into your daily work. Make sure you ride your pony properly at all times – so when schooling use the corners of your arena and do not let your pony fall into transitions.

Tip
Keep a diary of your pony's work, feed, competitions, visits to the farrier, vet etc – that way you should find it easier to remember vital details like regular worming, vaccinations and shoeing.

Fitness notes
Your pony needs to be fit for his job ie properly prepared for the work you ask him to undertake. He'll soon become bored if his days consist solely of practising gymkhana games. Take your pony for regular hacks out so he can encounter different sights and sounds, enjoy brisk canters along safe bridleways and learn obedience eg when opening gates etc without being in the confines of a schooling area.
Regular, slow work helps to build muscle and strengthen tendons.
If you live in a hilly area make good use of them – even walking briskly up a hill is quite hard work, so introduce it gradually.
Whether you're riding up or down hill try to ease your pony's back by taking your weight off him – hold onto his mane or a neckstrap if you find it difficult to keep your balance. Try not to interfere with his movement too much. When travelling downhill, keep an even contact and let your body go with the movement of the horse.

Over the next few weeks the amount of fast work can gradually build up and schooling can also include jumping. You need to allow at least eight weeks before your first competition to ensure that your pony is fit enough. It's better to allow more time in case anything happens to upset your plans, eg you may not be able to ride for a week due to influenza and so on.

Every pony and everyone's facilities are different, so you have to adapt the basic ideas to suit you and your pony. Perhaps someone else can help with the exercising, or lungeing the pony, if you're snowed under with school work. If you miss days in the early weeks do not try to make up for lost time by doing more work at the weekend – the pony needs his work to be built up gradually every day.

Add variety to your fitness programme by riding out with friends, or, if you normally ride in a group, by hacking out alone. However, always tell people where you are going and how long you expect to be out. It's such a simple thing to remember – and it can prevent a lot of unnecessary worry.

You can also make use of your hacks out to accustom your pony to moving away from other ponies and staying behind when asked. In

Mane pulling

Does your pony's mane resemble a thick, unruly mess? Then smarten him up for the show season by pulling his mane. This involves shortening and thinning out the mane so that it is more manageable.

You should aim to have a mane which is about 5 inches long and is level for the whole length of the pony's neck. Even if your pony lives out his mane can be pulled although it is kinder to leave his forelock long so he has some protection against flies around his eyes in summer.

Pull the mane after your pony has been exercised as his pores will be open and the hair will come out more easily. Never take hairs from the top of the mane or they'll simply grow back spiky.

First of all comb out the mane thoroughly so it is tangle free. Then, working on small sections of hair, take hold of the longest hairs which stem from the underside of the mane. Using the mane comb back-comb the rest of the mane upwards (ie towards the pony's crest). Then wind the long hairs around the mane comb, give a quick, sharp tug and pull the hairs out by the roots.

You must be careful not to try and remove too many hairs at a time. Some ponies object to having their manes pulled and others may soon start to play up if you overdo the mane pulling. Do not try to complete the job in one session – spread the pulling out over a few days so the pony does not get too sore.

Just take a little at a time, work your way down the mane, stopping to brush it out regularly so that you can see if you are keeping it level.

Clippers or scissors should not be used to shorten a mane. Clippers are used, however, if you hog a pony's mane ie remove it completely.

Top tip

To encourage your pony's mane to lie flat on the correct side of his neck (that's the pony's off side) keep dampening the mane using a water brush to make the hair lie flat. You can also plait it regularly to 'train' an unruly mane.

Tail tip

If you need to trim your pony's tail ask a friend to place his or her arm under the tail and hold it to the height the pony carries his tail when trotting. Then run your hand down the tail and cut it to the required length below the pony's hocks.

your stable yard or field teach your pony to lead readily in-hand at both walk and trot. Start off using a headcollar rather than a bridle as, if the pony decides to be stubborn and you try to drag him along, he may be bashed in the teeth by the bit. Once he's got the hang of moving alongside you without any hassle you can practise with his tack on.

Remember the value of your voice in encouraging him or soothing him if he starts to get excited in gymkhana practice sessions. Always keep your voice at an even level – there's no need or sense in shouting. Be patient with your pony and he will reward you.

Pre-show preparation

Whether you're entering a gymkhana race or a showing class a well turned out pony is a credit to his owner. If it's warm enough on the day before a show, you can bath your pony, although this is not an essential part of preparation.

White socks and stockings do tend to get stained so it's a good idea to wash your pony's white markings, using warm water, proper horse shampoo, as opposed to the ordinary human variety of shampoo, and a soft brush or sponge. Make sure you remove all the soap and if you are working around the sensitive areas of a pony, eg his eyes, sheath, dock, take extra care with the shampoo as you would not want to cause him any irritation.

Bathing tips
Always use a proper horse shampoo if you bath your pony – never ordinary human products! Be especially careful around the pony's eyes and ears – do not use soap on the face. Give your pony a bath on a warm day – never risk giving him a chill. Wash and rinse quickly so your pony does not catch cold and walk him around afterwards to dry.

Remember!
To keep at least two different sponges in your grooming box – one to be used for cleaning the pony's nostrils and the other for the dock.

If you can, stable him for the night before the show, as there's nothing worse than coping with a muddy, messy pony on show mornings. A deep clean bed helps and you could also kit the pony out in a light summer sheet to keep the majority of his body clean. His legs could be bandaged with stable bandages over gamgee as an extra method of ensuring cleanliness.

Once the pony has been attended to, turn your attention to your tack – it needs to be clean and safe, so when cleaning it check over the buckles and stitching. You should make safety checks whenever you clean your tack so that any repairs can be carried out quickly, well before show days and thus prevent accidents.

Next on the agenda are your clothes – you too need to be neatly turned out. Clean jodhpurs, white shirt, riding boots or jodhpur boots, plus a tie, are the usual outfit. If you're a Pony Club member wear your club tie. Don't forget the most essential item of your kit – your crash hat.

Fig 17 (left) A trace clip – perhaps lower than this if your pony spends a considerable amount of time outside – is one way of combating the need to work a pony quite hard but without removing all or too much of his coat
Fig 18 (right) A blanket clip

Timesaver
Whenever you pick out your pony's feet use a skep to collect the mud etc rather than letting it fall straight onto the floor or your pony's bed. After all, if you don't use a skep you'll only have to brush up the mud later.

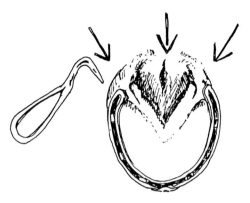

Fig 19 Always pick the pony's feet out using the hoof-pick from heel to toe

Gymkhana day

Try not to alter your pony's routine too much on show days or he may start to get excited in anticipation of something happening. If he's usually fed in the morning make sure he has plenty of time, ie about 20 minutes, to eat his feed before you start to get him ready.

Groom him, oil his hooves and kit him out in his travelling gear if you're boxing to the show. Check that all your equipment is packed away neatly in the lorry or car, ie tack, buckets, hay, first aid kit, grooming kit, clothes, a container of water, anti-sweat rug and so on.

If you are hacking to the event persuade a member of the family to transport your equipment to the show for you. Above all, whether you're riding over or travelling in style, allow yourself plenty of time to get ready and for the journey itself. Both you and your pony need to arrive in calm frames of mind and ready for the day's competition.

When you arrive at the show check that your pony is okay before finding out whether the show is running on time. Orientate yourself so that you know exactly where the gymkhana ring is, which area you

Tip
Although there is no need to plait your pony's mane and tail for
mounted games, make sure he is clean and tidy. By turning
yourself and your pony out to a high standard, you are paying the
show organisers a compliment.

can use for warming up, where the collecting ring entrance is, and
so on.

Allowing yourself enough time for all the necessary tasks, unload
your pony and remove his travelling gear. Brush him over, tack up
and fit any protective boots as necessary. Mount up and ride him
quietly around the showground so he can accustom himself to all the
sights and sounds before you ask him to concentrate on working in.

If your pony becomes excitable easily, choose the quietest corner
of the showground to work in. Plenty of circles, figures of eight and
transitions will give him enough to think about and take his mind off
the excitement of the occasion.

Plan your riding in so that you do not have to wait around too long
before you ride in the games. When you have finished your heats,
dismount, slacken the girth and give your pony a rest. Do not use
him as a grandstand seat to watch your friends compete and don't
race him around the showground, as you're only wasting his energy
and being very unfair to him.

If it's a hot day and your pony is sweaty he'll appreciate being
washed down – remember to bring enough water to do this and
have some left so that the pony can be offered a drink at suitable
intervals throughout the day. Let your pony cool down and dry off by
leading him around. Once he's okay you can prepare for the journey
home. If hacking home, adopt a steady gentle pace.

Top Tip
After working in hot weather your pony will appreciate being
washed down. Sponge him off and remove excessive water with a
sweat scraper.
In hot weather help to keep your pony more comfortable by
applying a fly repellent.

On arrival at home, no matter how tired you are, you must see to your pony's needs first. As you remove any travelling gear, check him over for any cuts or lumps that may have occurred, water and feed him before turning him out or bedding him down. Even if your pony is normally stabled he will appreciate the chance of a short while in his field after a show so that he can have a roll and relax.

Rules for gymkhanas

You would not enter a showjumping or working hunter class without checking on the rules for the particular event first, so it makes sense to familiarise yourself with the rules you'll come across when competing in gymkhanas.

The following are general rules that will apply unless otherwise stated in the rules for a particular show.

- Riders must be properly dressed and wearing the correct headgear. If your crash hat does come off(!), you must replace it before continuing with the game.
- Ponies must be properly turned out with saddles, bridles and stirrups. In events where saddles are not used, all martingales and neck straps must also be removed. The reins must be over and not under the pony's neck. Long reins can be knotted.
- No rider may enter more than one pony in an event, nor may a pony be entered by more than one rider in an event.
- A pony that is not properly under control, or kicks, is lame or is otherwise classed as unfit to be ridden, will not be allowed to compete.
- Whips and spurs are not allowed in gymkhana events.
- If a competitor is not in the collecting ring after being called three times he or she will be eliminated from the event.
- Except when the rules allow riders to dismount, they should remain mounted. The rider who falls off should remount and continue the event from the point of the fall.
- If a pony runs away loose from its rider it will be eliminated from the event.
- No rider may help another unless both are involved in a handover.
- A rider who receives outside assistance may be eliminated at the discretion of the chief judge. Where horse holders are used, or

stewards hand objects to riders, the riders must not be helped in any other way.

- In all races where the riders weave around bending poles the following applies:
  a) the riders may pass the first pole on either side; for the remainder they must weave alternately to the left and right
  b) riders are eliminated if they i) pass the wrong side of a pole and fail to correct the mistake ii) break a post so that it lies on the ground.
- A rider who dismounts to correct an error must hold the pony by the reins while doing so.
- A rider who drops an item that has to be carried, handed over or put into/taken out of a container, must dismount and pick it up again. The rider must then remount before resuming the race from the same point. However, at a handover in a pair or team event the next rider must pick it up.
- If an item drops out of, or bounces out of a container that the rider has placed it in, the rider must dismount immediately, pick it up, and then remount before putting the item back in the container.
- A rider who knocks over a container, table or post, must set it up again and replace all the items in it or on it; and must then remount before resuming the race; the penalty is elimination.
- Handovers from one rider to the next must take place behind the changeover line (with the whole of the next rider and pony being behind the line until the previous rider has crossed it, or until the baton or other item has been handed over).
- A rider who makes a mistake during an event may return to correct it, even after crossing the changeover line or finishing line, provided he or she has not left the arena or the race has not been declared over. A rider who goes back may not hand over or finish until the line has again been crossed after making the correction.
- Rough or dangerous riding, or deliberate interference, or bad behaviour, may be penalised by elimination of the rider.
- The result of a race is determined by the order in which the ponies' heads cross the finishing line for ridden finishes or by the order in which the riders cross the line when dismounted, eg in the sack race.

- Riders must leave the arena when they have finished their event, or part in an event, unless told otherwise by the judges.
- If the judges cannot decide on one or more of the placings in an event or heat the riders must run the event or heat again.
- Objections can only be lodged by the competitor, or by the parent or guardian of a competitor under 17 years of age. The objection must be in writing and accompanied by a deposit. If the objection is sustained, then the deposit is returned.

5
TRAVELLING

Every level of mounted games involves travel – for the newcomer to the sport journeys will be relatively short, taking in all the local shows, but at county team level travel involving 400-mile round trips may be necessary.

It's vital that the gymkhana pony travels well, without undue distress that might impair his performance in the ring. If your pony is not used to loading and travelling, it is wise to prepare him for this aspect of life well before the show season begins.

Loading

Ideally all ponies ought to be accustomed to loading at an early age. Correct early training can provide trouble-free loading for life but an improper introduction to loading and travelling can have long-lasting detrimental effects.

Never try to teach a pony anything if you're short of time – the inevitable result is an unsettled pony, an irate human and a backwards step so far as the pony's loading career is concerned.

Your trailer or horsebox needs to be as inviting as possible to your pony – and especially if the pony has never been loaded before or has bad memories of this particular part of life.

Remove the central partition altogether or move it across so that the pony has as large an area as possible. If the trailer is front unload, open the door so that the inside is light and airy. Lay a good bed of straw or shavings in the trailer and on the ramp if necessary, to assist grip.

It's a good idea to park the trailer so that one side is against a wall or fence – therefore the pony can only swerve out to one side. Put the trailer stabilisers down and position the box so that the ramp can be lowered onto level ground rather than onto an uneven surface. This is because if your pony puts his hooves onto the ramp and feels it move he can easily become frightened. Organise all this before you attempt to load the pony.

When loading, walk alongside the pony near his shoulder. As you've no doubt discovered, standing in front of a pony trying to pull him along just does not work. It's also dangerous to stand in front as, if the pony suddenly barged into the trailer, you could be knocked over and hurt. Wear gloves so that, if the pony pulls, your hands are protected from rope burn. It's also sensible to wear a hard hat, particularly if the pony is an unknown quantity when it comes to loading.

Whether you're teaching a pony to load for the first time or trying to re-educate a difficult loader you'll have to accept that loading lessons will need to be a regular occurrence. The pony needs to realise that there's nothing frightening about entering a trailer and indeed that the experience can be quite rewarding, ie the pony gets an edible treat.

If you have a young pony who is wary of the trailer, give him his feed off the trailer ramp, gradually moving the feed bowl up the ramp. The pony has to stand on the ramp to eat and before he knows it, he'll be happily eating away inside the trailer. How long this takes depends very much on the individual – from personal experience my youngster had no fears about going in a trailer on the first few occasions but some time later he did object, even though he had never had any bad experiences when travelling. Patience, however, did bring its rewards.

Once the pony is happy going into the trailer and unloading, preferably via a front unload ramp, you can accustom him to standing in the trailer with the back up. Talk to the pony, give him a haynet to pull at and leave him tied up in the trailer – but always with you very close at hand so that if he panics you can help immediately.

With the pony quite calm about everything so far, it's time to introduce him to travelling in the trailer. Keep the journeys short at first and try to avoid the routes that take in six roundabouts in quick succession. The pony should be kitted out adequately and the driver needs to take extra care (see later for help on these two aspects).

Gradually you can build up your pony's travelling time, take him to local shows or box him to a different area for a hack. Although this method takes time you should have a pony who is easy to load – and that can be a real blessing when the show's over, you're tired and just want a hasslefree journey home.

Difficult loaders
Unfortunately you may find yourself in the position of having to load a pony who is difficult. If a pony barges, then substitute a bridle for his headcollar with the extra precaution of a lunge rein attached to the bridle. This is so that if the animal pulls back he ought not to break free.

Even the smallest of ponies is incredibly strong when it does not want to do something, so it is no use trying to use your strength against a pony. Brains, not brawn, are required. It's also sensible to dissuade children from trying to cope with difficult loaders – adult helpers who are ponywise are necessary.

Try not to place yourself in a potentially dangerous position – even the calmest of ponies may launch into a kicking bout if upset about loading. You may find yourself inundated with offers of help from people who think they know it all but who succeed only in upsetting the pony and its attendant humans even more.

If a pony is being difficult to load, position the car and trailer so that everything is as safe as possible. Otherwise a pony may dive off the ramp and damage another car parked alongside; if you're parked close to a ditch or barbed wire you could have an injured pony and/ or handler – foresee any potential accident situations and avoid them.

For really awkward loaders you will need someone to lead and another two people to give encouragement from behind. Attach two lunge reins to either side of the trailer and then ask your helpers to cross these behind the pony as he approaches the ramp. The ropes should be positioned so that they apply pressure around the pony's quarters – be careful that they do not slip too low and become entangled with his feet.

The lunge lines can be used to keep the pony straight and to encourage him to move forwards up the ramp. If he does object strongly and panics the lines can always be loosened quickly to avoid any mishap. Encouragement can also be offered in the form of a bucket of feed to entice the pony into the trailer. You may also need to place his feet on the ramp.

Once the pony has given in and entered the trailer, make a fuss of him. And make sure you can devote some time to him in the near future to avoid a repeat of his difficult loading.

Travelling gear

No matter how long or short the journey, it makes sense to protect your pony from possible injury by kitting him out in boots and bandages.

Depending on the time of year and weather you may need rugs for your pony. Other gear includes a poll guard, knee caps and hock boots, protective boots or bandages for the legs, overreach boots, tail bandage and tailguard.

If a pony panics and throws up his head either as he enters a trailer or during travel, he can injure himself quite nastily. A poll guard is therefore a useful item of kit – it can be bought in a saddlers' or some people improvise and make their own.

Knee caps are a boon, especially if the pony is one who paws away while the trailer is parked. Remember to fit them so that the bottom strap allows for flexion of the knee.

Hock caps need to be fitted carefully so that they do not restrict movement – some horses and ponies tend to lean back against the trailer ramp and hock caps will protect against injury.

Travel checklist
Every time you travel your pony make sure he is wearing: poll guard; well fitting headcollar and serviceable lead rope; knee boots; hock boots; bandages over gamgee or travelling boots; tail bandage and tail guard; appropriate rugs.

There's a whole host of travelling boots and bandages on the market now – some incorporate protection for knees and hocks thus saving on the expense of buying separate boots. Whilst the boots are usually quick and easy to apply, the more traditional bandages, fitted over gamgee or another similar material, give more support. This is especially important if longer journeys are undertaken.

Some ponies tread on themselves during journeys, so it's a good idea to ensure that boots or bandages cover the coronary band and/ or fit overreach boots as an extra precaution.

Tail bandages help to prevent rubbed tails, while a tail guard offers extra protection – particularly if you find that your pony's tail bandage has slipped down during the journey. A stocking placed over the full length of the tail, before a bandage is applied, keeps the pony's tail clean.

Remember that bandages should not be left on for hours on end – tail bandages in particular should not be left on overnight or for long

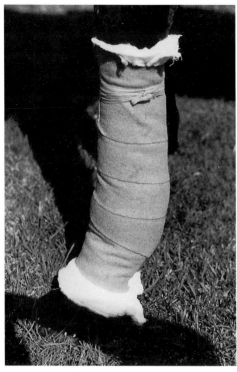

Protect your pony's legs when travelling . . . gamgee under stable bandages offer more support for longer journeys than travelling boots

periods. When removing bandages always rub the legs to help restore circulation.

Driving

One of the easiest ways to put a pony off loading for life is to let a bad driver tow a trailer. Anyone who is responsible for transporting ponies must show consideration for the animals throughout the whole journey.

You should aim for smoothness, particularly with gear changes and when slowing down for junctions or pulling away from traffic lights, etc. The driver needs to think ahead far more than when driving under normal circumstances in order to avoid any sudden braking or emergency stops. Extra care is needed around round-abouts and corners so that adequate clearance is given for both car and trailer.

If you are unused to towing, then take out the trailer, minus the pony, for some practice runs. That way you'll become used to the trailer length and width, how to negotiate bends, hills and corners, etc without the pony having to suffer for your inexperience.

Reversing is a difficult manoeuvre at first – in order to have the trailer moving in the correct direction you have to turn the steering wheel in the opposite direction to that in which you wish to go. It can take quite a while to become used to that way of thinking.

Your maximum speed is 60mph, although in practice you'll find that it is much slower – if you do go too fast, especially when travelling downhill, you may find yourself in a very frightening situation. The trailer may start to snake behind you and there is a danger of the trailer and the car being overturned. Slow down – but not by braking quickly. Instead, brake very gradually and hold the steering wheel straight – don't panic and don't get yourself into that situation again!

Longer journeys
Before you undertake any long journey, ie more than three hours or so, your pony must be accustomed to and happy with shorter trips in the trailer. Ensure that your car and trailer are fully roadworthy and that spare tyres are properly inflated before setting off.

Protect your pony with the appropriate travelling gear and ensure you have a good supply of food and water for him. Give him plenty

---

Travel tip

If you're travelling just one pony in a double horse trailer use the right hand side of the trailer (ie the side nearest the centre of the road). This usually gives the pony a better ride.

When towing adjust your speed according to conditions – it's completely different towing a live animal than an inanimate object such as a caravan. Do not be tempted to drive too fast, particularly if you are on motorways.

Choose your towing vehicle carefully – consult the car's manual for its safe towing weight. Your car must be able to stop safely in a towing emergency.

If you are lucky enough to own a horsebox your permitted travelling speed is dependent upon the weight and load. For a wealth of information on the whole subject of travelling a recently published book *Transporting Your Horse or Pony* by Chris Larter and Tony Jackson, is a superb investment.

---

of straw or other bedding on the trailer floor and let the pony have a good haynet to keep him occupied throughout the journey.

Make regular stops on the journey to check the pony and offer him water. If you hear any strange noises from the trailer stop and check – it's sensible to carry a first aid kit for both pony and humans. If you stop on the motorway services for food etc, try not to leave the pony alone.

At your destination unload the pony and lead him around so that he can stretch his legs after a long journey.

Insurance

Before you consider travelling with a pony you need to see that all possible eventualities are catered for. You'll need separate insurance for your car, trailer and pony. If another person is transporting your pony, make sure that insurance cover is still effective.

An organisation for owners of horseboxes and trailers that provides help in the case of accidents or emergencies may be contacted for more information at The Organisation of Horsebox and Trailer Owners, Organisation House, 38 Newton Road, London W2 5LT.

Trailer and horsebox care

As these items entail considerable financial investment they should be looked after properly and regularly checked for safety reasons. Every time a trailer or lorry is used, make sure that you check the basics, eg tyres, spares, electrics, braking system and so on. After the show clean out the dirty bedding and let the floor air. With older trailers in particular check that the floor is sound. Grease the moveable parts of the central partition and breast bars – there's nothing worse than struggling to get pins and bolts home.

Check that the ramp springs are in good order, that the brake linkage is well lubricated, that the electrical connections are clean and sound, especially after a journey when the trailer has been through wet, muddy terrain.

Whatever you're doing with ponies, whether it's travelling or schooling, think ahead, prepare and you'll be in the best position to cope with any untoward event.

6
A MOUNTED
GAMES YEAR

When it comes to the Prince Philip Cup Mounted Games, one of the Pony Club branches that, year after year, throws down the gauntlet to all other teams, is the Wylye Valley branch.

Having qualified for Wembley on eight occasions out of twelve and won the highly valued event twice, it is, without a doubt, a force to be reckoned with.

Team trainer George Marshall firmly believes his A team will continue to carry on the tradition so long as there are mounted games at the Horse of the Year Show.

Reaching the final is not an easy task, and it's only the best who earn a place in the qualifying teams. It is to George's credit that his branch of the Pony Club has a team there most years.

The preparation for the annual mounted games begins in November when district commissioners, team trainers, stewards, parents and all who want to know more, or to be involved with the mounted games, attend a study day at the Pony Club Headquarters at Stoneleigh in Warwickshire.

At the study day the games committee tells those concerned what games will be held for the area and zone finals as well as at the final. The rules for newly introduced games are explained, as well as demonstrations, so that those present know exactly what needs to be done for the season.

Following that, training starts in January with a schedule of events. In the case of the Wylye Valley, the district commissioner invites all the youngsters interested in competing in the games to bring their ponies to a certain venue.

He or she will then tell the children what is expected of them, what games and rules there are for the area and zone finals, the techniques to be used, and so on.

The parents are also invited to hear the 'implications' of the mounted games year. George feels that the support of the parents is imperative for children who tackle the sport.

'Without the parents' enthusiasm and dedication, the riders do not have much of a chance of being in the team,' said George, 'for it is the parents who have to transport their children here, there and everywhere.

'We need to know that children will turn up for their training, their home competitions and away finals. We cannot have a rider turning up at one event, and not coming to the next two. The games

Despite all the excitement of the races the ponies must be obedient at all times (Horse & Pony Magazine)

themselves demand a team and a dedicated team at that.'

Dedication may be a priority for a team member but he or she also, according to George, needs to be of the right temperament, have the ability to ride well, be athletic, have courage and also be able to work with a team.

'We do get some children who are very good riders but who have no regard for team effort. It is imperative that the youngsters who compete for the Prince Philip Cup are able to work closely as a team.'

A good mounted games pony does not need to cost a fortune, says George. 'Most of the ponies we have in the Wylye Valley are ordinary ponies, which cost between £200 and £300 to buy. However, once they are trained, the price does tend to go up.'

George feels that a good 40 per cent of all children's ponies could make Prince Philip Cup teams. So what does he look for in a pony for his team? 'It must not be too big, as the child needs to operate on as small a pony as possible. It makes life easier when picking up objects, items, articles etc, and vaulting on and off. On saying that, you must match the pony with the rider. There is little point in putting a long-legged girl on a very small pony – it would look ridiculous and would not be a good combination.'

George's ideal pony is 12.3hh with plenty of bone and substance – preferably of Welsh or Connemara type. 'The ponies must be unflappable, well-schooled and fit. They must also be willing and enthusiastic – like people, if they do not have the enthusiasm they will not do a good job.'

George also has a preference for geldings – 'geldings are more predictable and stable, especially when it comes to pairs' racing. I would like to see more geldings as opposed to mares, although if you get a good mare she's worth her weight in gold.'

The first six weeks of the new year are taken up with training both riders and their ponies, and getting the ponies fit. 'I do like them to school their ponies for half an hour each day,' stressed George, who realises that January and February are not easy months in which to ride because of the weather and light.

However, a child competitive enough to aim at Wembley must be prepared to work for it. During these initial training sessions riders learn to vault correctly, a technique that is quite difficult and demands a certain amount of courage.

With between twenty and forty riders requiring training and vying for places in the Wylye team, George certainly has his work cut out.

'We have a junior as well as a senior team. The juniors, our B team, compete in mounted games competitions like our seniors, the A team.

'The B team is aimed at youngsters 12 years and under. The riders picked for this team enter local competitions and graduate to a national competition, which is held at Aston Court in Bristol, for the Prince Philip Mounted Games Trophy, also a prestigious annual event.'

By the time March has arrived, George has made his decision as to the six he recommends entering for the junior and senior teams to represent the Wylye Valley. The sixth member is a reserve.

'From then on we polish up the particular games, ready for the area competitions in the Easter holidays.' In particular, George likes the children to brush up on their handover techniques, vaulting and their speed.

A MOUNTED GAMES YEAR

'We tend to put the pressure on our A team by expecting them to do a little more each time they practise. We use a stop watch on them for the competitive games. The juniors we are less harsh on, as they are younger and need to be brought on more slowly.'

On saying that, George stresses that things are not rushed; far from it – as no problems are resolved in haste.

As the competitions loom, the riders carry out their training and inter-competitions not just every weekend but also twice in the week, in addition to doing their own riding and schooling in any spare time.

Once the area finals are over, if the team's successful – and, says George, it's a rare occasion that it's not – the team gets a well deserved rest for two weeks.

Training recommences after the break and the Wylye Valley team takes part in as many competitions as possible in the build-up to the zone finals, including the popular Bath & West Show.

At this show twelve teams compete over a four-day period in the Prince Philip Cup games that they will undertake in the zone finals.

And when not out and about competing, the team practises at home, perfecting its techniques.

Fun and teamwork is the hallmark of the Games – epitomised here by the Bramham Moor team (Basil Birchall)

'Normally the team that takes part in the area finals goes forward to the zone finals,' said George, 'but on occasions we have substituted one rider for another.' George is keen on switching the ponies and riders around to find the most suitable combinations – 'the children do not necessarily have to ride their own ponies to make the best team.'

But it's not all mounted games competitions as George firmly believes in the adage 'variety is the spice of life' and encourages the children to take part in many other Pony Club events, including cross-country and tetrathlons.

'It's good for the riders and good for the ponies who tend to go stale if they do the same thing all the time.'

By the end of the zone finals the six qualifying teams have been chosen to go to Wembley, but the runners-up do not just slip away. They have another competition at the National Carriage Driving Championships at Harrogate.

The area and zone finals over, the Wembley finalists have two weeks off before they carry on, in much the same vein as before. This time, however, they practise the games they will be playing at Wembley, following instructions received from the Pony Club's Mounted Games Committee.

Wembley – the ultimate occasion for the Pony Club mounted games competitors
(Horse & Pony Magazine)

'The teams compete in twenty-eight events at the Horse of the Year Show,' said George, 'so what we do, if chosen, is to start practising the newly introduced games outside first, before venturing inside to try and capture the Horse of the Year Show atmosphere.

'We turn the music on, have lots of noise and attempt to re-create the Wembley arena. We carry this on right up to October.'

Wembley beckoning, the teams arrive complete with ponies, tack, clothing, food, bedding for the ponies and feed, veterinary and medical products (just in case), buckets, grooming kits – the list goes on and on.

When the entourage arrives, and before the ponies are stabled and their needs attended to, the team trainer has to produce up-to-date vaccination certificates for the animals. Following that, the teams find their appropriate rooms for the duration of the show – inevitably caravans on the showground.

The girls and boys are housed in separate caravans, although they all take their meals together with the team trainer and district commissioner.

The children become involved in more than mounted games. They have a competition to find the best kept stable and tack room, for which a trophy is awarded to the winning team.

Most of the youngsters enlist the help of friends and family in turning the tack room into something quite special, as they have to find a theme which is horse orientated.

'The teams never know when the judges will turn up to assess their work,' said George, 'and they do not know who the judges will be.'

The judges take into consideration all manner of things when determining the winning team. The bedding is checked, the care of the ponies, in fact all the things you'd expect a stable yard to be has to be evident. And of course they consider the tack room and its theme to be equally important.

It's not all work either. The riders, once they've tended to their ponies and done some training (which, according to George, is restricted due to the lack of space), cleaned tack etc, take time off to enjoy other aspects of the show before taking part themselves, 'there are just not enough hours in a day at the show.'

Before the riders compete they are given the colours that are provided by the sponsors of the event.

Mounted games go international: the British team of (left to right) Matthew Peacock, South Down West; Jane Brown, Eglington; Anita Barber (coach); Iain Hopkins, Clydach & District; Katie Reid, South Wold North and Helen Marshall, Bramham Moor, who triumphed over teams from Canada and the USA in a 1987 event (Basil Birchall)

Once the afternoon competitions are over, the children and the ponies attended to, the riders can relax and enjoy each other's company before they have to get ready for the evening performance.

It all sounds terribly easy but, according to George, things don't always go according to plan. The most common fault seems to be panic – the rider does something wrong and is quite amazed, despite the months spent practising and competing against other teams.

'However, competing at Wembley is unlike anything else. The adrenalin is going, the atmosphere is totally different and the ponies sense it. Children sometimes panic and make mistakes.

'They do things in a heat that they would never normally do and have never done before. They have already been taught to operate under pressure and become disciplined to do things automatically, so we don't generally have too many problems – or panics.'

The Prince Philip Cup Mounted Games are put on to entertain the audience and that is made quite clear by the master of the Wembley Games, Raymond Brooks-Ward.

'He likes the games to cause hilarity for the crowds,' commented the Wylye Valley trainer. 'It's also made clear that the teams are there to entertain the public, not solely for the competing. It has a show business ring about it and is not to be taken quite so seriously – to get to Wembley is an award in itself.'

Part of the pleasure of getting to Wembley is the immense excitement particularly when the teams win their heats, taking them forward to the final night. If they have had a successful night they will parade around the arena with the spotlight on them – that is a memory those children will treasure forever. Not to mention the memory that the team carrying off the Prince Philip Cup will hold!

7
RUNNING A
GYMKHANA

Organising a village gymkhana can either be an enormous headache or a great deal of fun. Its success will depend, to a large extent, on a committee, voluntary helpers, sponsors and attention to detail. Very often gymkhanas are combined with a show so that there is literally 'something for everyone'.

Behind every good gymkhana is a hard working committee. You will need at least six people and three of these should be appointed to hold the posts of chairman, secretary and treasurer. Forward planning is essential. Most committees plan a year in advance as sponsors need to be found, a field has to be begged, borrowed or hired from a local farmer, equipment has to be hired or bought – the list seems endless. Each member of the committee should be assigned various tasks to fulfil.

The date and number of classes must be decided upon and a venue selected. You will probably find a friendly local farmer who will help out with a field for the event – one may even let you have the field for nothing provided you leave it as you found it, clearing away all litter and equipment.

The programme should be planned to include a variety of events to suit the ages and experience of the potential competitors. You must remember to order enough rosettes, usually to sixth place, well in advance.

Insurance is something that must not be forgotten. Your committee is strongly advised to insure against claims – cover for public liability and contractual liability should be sought. The latter applies if you use rented or borrowed premises.

There are numerous insurance companies that will be only too pleased to offer a service and the British Horse Society also arranges insurance. It is a good idea to include a disclaimer in your programme.

Prevention, as they say, is better than cure – and you should arrange for the local St John Ambulance Brigade to provide cover for the duration of the event. A payment is required for this so remember to include it in your expenses budget. Book a farrier and a vet too – they may be on standby duty.

The schedule should include the name and address of the organiser or secretary, the date, time and venue of the gymkhana and show, as well as the entry fees and prizes.

A budget has to be prepared and this is where your sponsors are

SORBROOK HORSE SHOW & GYMKHANA

Sunday May 10, 1987

9.30am prompt
in the field along Tillie's Lane
by kind permission of Mr I. L. Walkes

ENTRIES ON THE FIELD

JUMPING: Cups to be won, rosettes to 6th place
GYMKHANA: Rosettes to 6th place
PAIRS RELAY: Cup & rosettes

BAR
RAFFLE
REFRESHMENTS
ST JOHN AMBULANCE

Admission:
CHILDREN 20p   ADULTS 35p   CARS & OCCUPANTS £1

Ring 1   9.30 prompt   JUMPING

CLASS 1   Not exceeding 12.2hh   *Entry fee 80p*
               Rider 12yrs & under

CLASS 2   Not exceeding 13.2hh   *Entry fee 80p*
               Rider 14yrs & under

CLASS 3   Not exceeding 14.2hh   *Entry fee 80p*
               Rider 16yrs & under

CLASS 4   Novice   *Entry fee £1*
               (Horse/Pony not to have
               won more then £5)

CLASS 5   Open   *Entry fee £1*

Time permitting: Open Scurry over   *Entry fee 70p*
                  3ft fences

Ring 2   9.30 prompt

               Clear Round Jumping   *Entry fee 50p*
               (Close at 2pm)

2pm   Mini Jumping   *Entry fee 60p*
               Rider 8yrs & under, Pony
               12.2hh & under (can be
               led)

3pm   **GYMKHANA**
               12.2hh & under (can be   *Entry fee 30p each event*
               led)
               1 Bending

2 Post A Letter

3 Cup Race

13.2hh & under
1 Tyre Race

2 Apple Bobbing

3 Fancy Dress Race

14.2hh & under
1 Cup Race

2 Bending

3 Sack Race

Open
1 Bending

2 Apple Bobbing

3 Sack Race

Ring 3   9.30 prompt   SHOWING

CLASS 6	Working Hunter Pony, 14.2hh & under	*Entry fee £1*
CLASS 7	Working Hunter, over 14.2hh	*Entry fee £1*
CLASS 8	Riding Horse, (no jumping)	*Entry fee £1*

Ring 4   9.30am to 3pm   HANDY PONY

SECTION 1	10yrs & under	*Entry fee 50p*
SECTION 2	Over 10yrs to 16yrs & under	*Entry fee 50p*

Rules of the show

1 No sticks or spurs allowed in any gymkhana event.

2 The judges' decision is final. Officials only in the ring. Height of fences are the judges' decision.

3 No responsibility can be taken for any damage or injury to animals, competitors, spectators or vehicles whatsoever.

4 Competitors must not canter around the outside of the rings, or they will be asked to leave the field.

5 No jeans, plimsolls or soft shoes allowed in any event.

6 Objections must be made to the secretary within 30 minutes of the incident, in writing, accompanied by a deposit of £3, returnable if the objection is sustained.

7 If a competitor is not in the collecting ring after being called three times, he or she will be eliminated from the event and no money refunded.

8 The committee reserves the right to alter, limit or cancel any class.

9 No competitor may ride more than two horses/ponies in any one event.

PLEASE DO NOT LEAVE LITTER
ALL DOGS ON LEADS AT ALL TIMES

COMMITTEE

Miss H. Russell (Chairman)   Miss S. Haw
Miss L. Maddox (Secretary)   Mr A. Wright
Mrs M. Hazlewood (Treasurer)   Mrs M. Coleman
Mrs A. Stroud   Mr V. Shrapnel

The Committee would like to thank Mr I. L. Walkes for the use of his fields and would also like to thank the sponsors:

SPONSORS:

Olympia Transport   H & P Designs
Grange Farm Ltd   Mr & Mrs D. A. Bannister
Country Dairies   The Bear Inn
                The Tack Shop

Determination from the rider and staying power by the leader are needed!

vital. The more sponsorship you can obtain, eg to offset the cost of rosettes, prize money and so on, the less money the committee will have to find to finance the event. If sponsors wish to give cups or some other form of trophies, these should be ordered well in advance, particularly if any is to carry the sponsor's name. Work out how much you are likely to spend, eg on printing schedules, rosettes, refreshments for the judges, hiring public address system, etc.

Once you have drawn up your programme you must decide how many copies you need before ordering from the printers. Publicity and advertising also need to be taken care of; although a lot of your publicity will be via word of mouth, it is also useful to advertise your event in the local newspaper, on posters in shop windows, riding schools, even in the back windows of cars!

Refreshments are next on the agenda – arrange for an outside caterer to attend the event, or perhaps a village resident or group could provide food and drink.

At all stages of organising a gymkhana an abundance of voluntary helpers is needed, so enlist the co-operation of your friends, their friends and anyone else you can persuade to 'muck in'.

Novice gymkhanas organised by a small committee for local riders are always popular

Parents get just as involved as the competitors!

Once you have been allocated a suitable field, which should be reasonably flat, rope off your sections for the gymkhana events and show. Borrow a tractor to transport the equipment, or a van big enough to hold everything.

Remember that adequate space is needed for parking horse boxes, cars, for a warm-up area, collecting ring, secretary's box or tent, commentary box and catering facilities.

The night before the gymkhana erect signposts along the route to help those riders coming from a distance to find the venue easily. Don't forget to remove the signs immediately after the show.

Officials need to be briefed on their various duties, which could be anything from collecting the admission fee at the gate to making sure that the competitors abide by the rules of each individual game. It's essential that anyone judging a gymkhana game is fully conversant with the rules.

The secretary's tent/caravan must be fully staffed at all times and well in advance of the starting time of the first class.

Organisation and delegation are the keywords. The chairman or organiser must be thinking and planning ahead as well as concentrating on what is happening immediately. It's a tall order but a necessary one if things are to run smoothly and efficiently.

The first event must be started on time – failure to do so will undoubtedly lead to the rest of the day's activities being late. Competitors then, understandably, become rather fed up.

Usually, entries are taken on the day at the local gymkhana – and normally attract large numbers. It can become quite confusing for the steward at the entrance to the arena – especially if he has to collect each competitor's money and give them an entry ticket. It's therefore a good idea to have a small collecting ring near the gymkhana arena which is divided into two sections. The entrances are controlled by stewards and competitors pay their entrance fees for the individual events before moving into the second half of the ring. This way you can take entries for each game right to the last minute without having to delay heats while someone finds the secretary's tent, pays and returns with the tickets.

After each game the ring needs to be cleared before entries can be taken for the next game.

Judging the heats is quite a formidable task and requires several stewards – it would be impossible to decide on the order of placing with just one judge to watch the proceedings.

The race commences once the starter has either dropped his flag or blown a whistle. Starters should stand to one side of the arena within 10 to 12yd (9 to 11m) of the riders. Once he is satisfied the riders are lined up correctly the starter will give the signal. If a pony plays up, thus delaying a start, the rider may be asked to hold the pony behind the line of the other competitors. If there is a false start the starter will raise his flag and recall the riders.

The judges need to be informed as to the winning riders from each heat and a steward should take down the names and numbers of the eligible riders to ensure there are no disputes over who rides in the final. At the end of each heat a duplicate copy of the results should be taken to the commentator's box so that he can announce which riders are needed for the final. The secretary also should be informed of the winners of each game.

It's wise to remind competitors that consideration should be shown towards their ponies. Some riders regard shows as a good opportunity to charge around for a few hours at high speed with little regard for their ponies. Everyone can have fun, without over-taxing the ponies. Ask riders to avoid unnecessary galloping, to dismount and loosen off girths so that ponies can be rested in between their classes.

Games at local gymkhanas

Some of the more popular gymkhana games at local shows are listed below with a few tips on general ringcraft and for the individual games:

The start: some games are started with a whistle while others, like the Prince Philip Cup games, are started with a flag. If it's a whistle start, keep your eye on the official starter as you can often see his cheeks blow out and so can gain a good getaway from the line.

Try to keep your pony on a reasonably loose rein at the start. Many competitors make the mistake of pulling on the pony's mouth, simply because they are anxious and nervous. This will only serve to get the pony het up, and while you are trying to kick the pony on and make him do what you want him to, your fellow competitors will have set off at great speed.

The finish: throughout the race concentrate on what you are doing, not what your opponents are up to. Many riders start looking around them to see what's happening in the next lane and whether they're being beaten. Don't! Concentrate on the job in hand. If you're riding to the best of your ability and your pony is giving of his best, there's nothing more you can do at that particular moment.

Bending race

Usually five poles are placed 6 to 10yd (5.5 to 9m) apart. For Prince Philip Cup games the poles are usually 10yd (9m) apart, as some of the games require pairs of ponies to 'bend' but for local shows the poles are usually set at the shorter distance.

Bending means weaving in and out of the poles, going along the line, then turning around and bending back again. A great deal of time can be lost on the turn. To avoid taking a wide berth around the last pole, go slightly away from it as you approach and then come tight back on it as you make the turn. Use your weight aids around the poles, leaning with the pony.

Flag race

For this competitors have to transfer two to four flags, attached to canes, from one container at the far end of the gymkhana ring to another container at the top.

How you hold the flag is important. Take hold of it as normal, but as you canter down to the next container turn it over, so that it points down and your index finger is running down the cane shaft. You'll find it easier to place the cane in the container. It's also vital to lean well down so that you can push the flag home into the container, rather than sitting bolt upright, dropping the flag in the vicinity of the container and hoping for the best!

When you reach the last flag remember to steady your pony as, if he's done this game a few times before, he may start to anticipate the gallop for the finish. Make sure the flag goes into the holder – after all it could be the difference between winning and losing.

Potato race

In this race you have to transfer several potatoes from a container on an oil drum or similar object to a bucket. As with the flag race, accuracy in depositing the item is essential. The riders need to be agile so they can lean down easily.

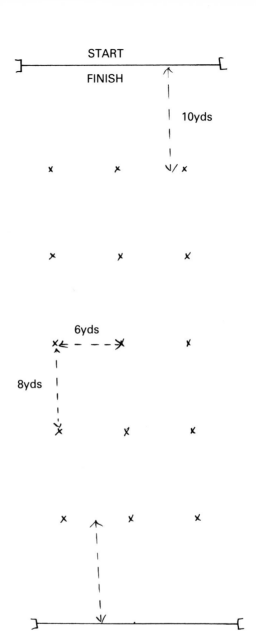

Fig 20 Suggested distances for a bending race layout

Stepping stone dash

The 'stones' are usually upturned buckets or cans and competitors are expected to canter down to the 'stones', dismount, cross the stones without turning any of them over and then vault back onto the pony to ride for the finishing line.

Vaulting on will take some time to perfect but it helps if you keep alongside your pony's shoulder rather than getting left behind. Your left hand goes onto the mane, while the right hand goes on to the pommel of the saddle. As your pony will be moving so you will be carried forward by the momentum of the pony. Run alongside, spring and throw your right leg over the saddle. Don't throw both legs into the air – you'll just end up in an uncomfortable heap, probably on the other side of the pony!

Cup race

You may find different variations on this. Some gymkhana organisers place three cups, usually plastic beakers, on the first three poles in a line of bending poles. The object is to move each cup up a pole, one at a time. Pick the cup up between your thumb and first finger, rather than making a grab for it, as this will give you more flexibility when placing it on the next pole. At other gymkhanas you are simply required to collect the cups.

Musical sacks

A popular game that operates on the same principles as the children's party game, musical chairs. There's always one more competitor than the supply of sacks. Riders move around the sacks in a large circle until the music stops. Then they dismount and lead their ponies to claim an empty sack. The rider who cannot find a sack is eliminated. Large heats can be reduced more quickly by removing two sacks at a time. Riders must keep their eyes on the position of the sacks and life is much easier if your pony leads well.

Egg and spoon race

An egg, hardboiled, is placed on a table at the far end of the arena. The rider, carrying a spoon, gallops to the table, picks up the egg without touching it by hand and then gallops to the finish with the egg on the spoon. If the egg falls off the table the rider must pick it up by hand, put it back on the table and pick it up again using the spoon before continuing with the race.

Similarly, if the rider drops the egg on the return journey then the rider must dismount and pick up the egg, resuming the race from the place where the egg was dropped.

Gretna Green race
This race is carried out in pairs. The equipment needed is a curtain ring placed on a chair midway down the arena plus pencil and paper on a table or barrel at the end of the arena, but positioned well before the finishing line.

The riders gallop to the chair, one rider dismounts, picks up the curtain ring, hands it to his team mate and remounts. They then both gallop to the table where they both must dismount, sign the 'register', remount and head for the finishing line which they cross hand in hand.

Laundry stakes
Another race for pairs. Position a set of laundry in a basket with two pegs for each article at the front of the arena and a washing line at the far end. One rider has to gallop with the laundry to the line, hanging up each article by two pegs. He then gallops back to the start and hands the basket to the second rider who collects the laundry and returns it, complete with pegs, to the finish.

Fancy dress race
A popular game, this requires sets of fancy dress. Each rider has to gallop to the far end of the arena, dismount, hand his pony to a steward, dress up, remount and gallop back to the finish.

Tyre race
A tyre is needed for each competitor and this is placed at the far end of the arena. Once riders have reached the tyres they dismount, hand their ponies to a steward and pass through the tyres before remounting and galloping for the finish.

Sack race
Each rider gallops to the far end of the arena, dismounts, gets into a sack and, leading the pony alongside, hops back to the finish.

It's easier to run in a sack if you make sure your feet are well into each corner of the sack

Wheelbarrow race

A race for two competitors – the first rider gallops to the end of the arena where the team mate waits, sitting in a wheelbarrow. The first rider dismounts, hands the reins to the team mate and proceeds to push the wheelbarrow back to the finish, while the other competitor leads the pony.

Shirt race

This can be run with individuals or in pairs. Large shirts with no buttons are needed. For an individual race, the rider gallops to the shirt, dismounts, puts the shirt on, remounts and heads back to the finish.

With the pairs, one rider starts off wearing the shirt. He has to gallop to his partner who is waiting, dismounted, with her pony at the far end of the arena. The first rider must dismount, take off the shirt and hand it to the second rider who puts it on, mounts and then

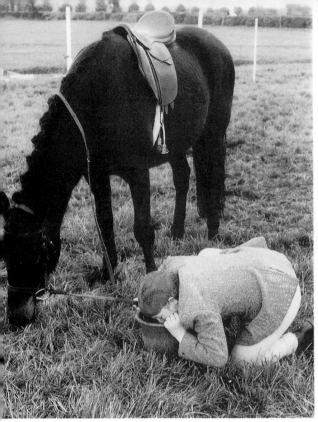

*Apple bobbing – you can spend ages chasing the apple around the bucket . . .
unless you manoeuvre the apple to the side of the bucket so you can sink
your teeth in . . . success!*

gallops back to the finish. Riders are allowed to help each other
when changing the shirt.

Saddling up race
Saddles are positioned at the far end of the arena. Riders gallop
bareback, dismount, saddle up, remount and then gallop back. The
first one to cross the line, with feet in the stirrups, wins.

Lucky dip race
Tubs or buckets are needed, filled with bran or straw, and containing
four differently shaped items plus a matchbox. Riders gallop to the
tubs, dismount and search for the matchbox. Once they've found it,
they remount and head for the finishing line.

Apple bobbing
Buckets are filled with water, and an apple floated in each one. Riders gallop to the buckets, dismount and try to take the apple out of the water – in their teeth! They then gallop back to the finishing line, apples in mouths (see above).

Litter race
Items of litter, eg plastic mugs or cartons are distributed on the ground at the far end of the arena while buckets are placed in the middle of the gymkhana lanes. Canes measuring 3 to 4 ft (.9 to 1.2m) are supplied to each rider who has to gallop to the litter, pick up an object with the cane, not with the hands, and transfer it to the bucket. Once the lane's litter has been picked up, the rider can cross the finishing line.

Handkerchief race
This race is for pairs and you will need a post with a man's

handkerchief tied to it at the far end of the arena as well as four bending posts, for each pair.

The pairs wend their way through the bending posts, untie the handkerchief and return through the posts, both holding the handkerchief, to the finish. If one rider lets go of the handkerchief, the pair must return to the point where the mishap happened before carrying on.

Musical mounting
For this race you need to position eight posts to form a large circle. When the music plays the riders trot or canter around this circle but as soon as the music stops they dismount on the near-side, run around the front of their ponies and mount on the off-side. The last rider up is eliminated and the game continues until there is only one person, ie the winner, left.

Balloon race
Two balloons attached by string should be fixed to a post midway along the arena and two more balloons fixed to a post at the far end. Riders go first to the far end, grab a balloon, return to the post halfway along the arena, collect a second balloon and gallop to the finish carrying both balloons. A rider who loses a balloon can attempt to retrieve it or simply collect another one from the post.

Uncle Tom Cobley stakes
Four bending poles are needed for this race, which should be ridden in pairs. The first rider gallops bareback through the bending poles to the second rider who is waiting, dismounted, at the far end. When the mounted rider arrives, the second competitor leaps aboard the pony and both gallop back to the finish.

8
PONY CLUB
GAMES

The Pony Club Mounted Games Committee is constantly introducing new games into the area and zone finals of the Prince Philip Cup as well as into the ultimate final at Wembley. Every year sees different games at the events, mixed in with the tried and trusted favourites.

Teams aiming for a place in the coveted final at the Horse of the Year Show will need to be super-competent in a number of games, which can include the following:

Team relay bending race
This race needs lines of bending poles, situated between 24 to 30ft (7 to 9m) apart. The first team member carries a baton and on the signal to start weaves down and back through the bending poles. On returning to the start the baton is handed to the next team member.

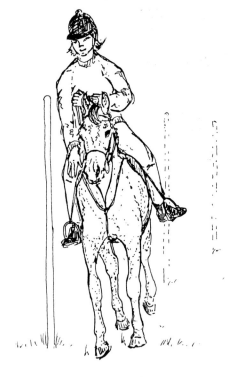

Fig 21 Get in close to the bending poles, leaning in as you would when riding a bicycle around a corner

The second, third and fourth members of the team repeat the procedure and the winning team is the one whose fourth member crosses the line first, mounted and carrying the baton.

The postman's chase

Bending poles are again required. Four letters are also needed, made from hardboard and measuring 8 by 4in (20 by 10cm). Sacks complete the equipment list.

The fifth member of each team stands with the letters 6yd (5.5m) behind the changeover line. Carrying a sack, the first team member gallops through the bending poles and across the changeover line to receive a letter from the fifth member. Number one places this letter in the sack, returns through the bending poles to the start and hands the sack to the second team member.

The other team members collect letters and the fourth member has to gallop for the finish, carrying all four letters in the sack.

Ball and cone race

Two cones are needed as well as a tennis ball for each team. The start and finish line are the same line at one end of the marked out arena with the changeover line at the other end. Place the two cones 15yd (13.5m) from either end with the ball positioned on the far cone.

Team members one and three should be at the start line while numbers two and four are stationed at the changeover line. Number one carries a tennis ball and, when signalled to start, gallops to the first cone, places the ball on it and then continues on to the second cone, collects the tennis ball and hands this to the second team member. Numbers two, three and four complete the course in a similar manner.

The last person to go must cross the finishing line carrying a tennis ball.

The old sock race

Four old socks are needed for each team. The socks should be sewn into balls about the size of a fist and placed within a circle marked on the ground. A row of buckets, one for each team, should be placed across the centre of the arena.

The first competitor in the team carries a sock, gallops to the team's bucket, drops the sock into it and then carries on to the far

Fig 22 Accuracy is improved by the rider's agility and ability to bend down without disturbing the pony's balance

end of the arena where the rider dismounts, picks up a sock, leaps back on the pony and returns to the start to hand over the sock to the next team member.

The game is over once all the socks have been dropped into the bucket and the fourth team member has crossed the line.

Two flag race
Each team needs two flag holders, situated 15yd (13.5m) from each end and one flag. Two members wait at the start line and two at the changeover line.

Number one member carries a flag, gallops to the first holder, puts the flag into it, then gallops to the second flag container, takes a flag out of this and hands it to the second rider. Number two repeats the procedure going back down the arena, handing over to the third team member and so on.

If the flag comes off the cane, it is acceptable to continue the race using just the cane.

Fishing race
Litter bins and 'fish', made from wood or plastic and measuring approximately 15in (40cm) long and 7in (18cm) wide, are needed.

Team member number five stands at the changeover line holding a post 4ft (1.2m) high with a crosspiece containing four hooks screwed into the underside.

The first rider who has a stick about 3ft (.9m) long with a small hook on one end, gallops to the litter bin, hooks a fish and continues on to the fifth member, carefully carrying the fish on the stick. Number five has to unhook the fish and secure it on a hook.

The first team member remains behind the changeover line until the fish has been correctly placed on the post and then returns to the start line to hand the fishing stick to the second contestant.

A rider who drops a fish may retrieve it either mounted or dismounted. The fifth team member can pick up the fish if it is dropped by a rider who has crossed the changeover line.

The Spillers' hurdle race

Four hurdles about 30in (75cm) wide are needed for this particular event. These should be placed 6ft (1.8m) apart positioned so that the hurdles are alternately 1ft (30cm) and 2ft (60cm) high. A mug, with a band of coloured tape around the top to correspond with each team, is placed on top of each hurdle.

The first two team members line up, side by side, on the start line with the number fours behind them. The third team rider waits on the changeover line.

When the signal to start is given, numbers one and two gallop to the hurdles where the first rider dismounts and hands her pony to her companion. She then has to step over the first hurdle, crawl under the next, leap over the third and under the fourth. Then she remounts. Both riders gallop over the changeover line and the first team member stays there.

The second team member does an 'about turn' and gallops back to the hurdles accompanied by the third rider. Number two contestant dismounts, negotiates the hurdles, remounts the pony, crosses the start line and drops out of the race.

The third rider turns around and, accompanied by the fourth team member, gallops to the hurdles. The third team member goes over and under the hurdles this time. He then drops out once they've crossed the line while the fourth team member, together with the first rider, makes the final trip, with the fourth rider tackling the hurdles.

The winning team is the one whose final pair crosses the finishing line first. At each changeover the next pony to go has to stay behind the line until both the previous ponies have crossed it. The rider whose turn it is to hold the pony at the hurdles may grasp the reins before, or as the riders gallop along the arena.

If a hurdle is knocked over, or a mug topples, the competitor must replace it and renegotiate the obstacle.

The rope race

Place lines of four bending poles 24 to 30ft (7 to 9m) apart. Two riders are at one end of the arena and two at the opposite end. Rider number one carries a rope about 3ft (90cm) in length.

The rider then gallops through the bending poles to the other end of the arena where the second contestant takes hold of the other end of the rope. Together they then return via the bending poles, each holding one end of the rope.

Once back at the start, the first competitor relinquishes the end of the rope to the third member. The riders then return through the bending poles to the far end of the arena where the second team member lets go of the rope and the fourth member grasps it. These two riders then make the final journey.

Should one of the riders let go of the rope while on the course both must return to the spot where the rope was dropped and resume the race.

Pyramid race

Two tables and four plastic cartons are needed for each team. Place one table halfway down the arena and the other at the changeover line. Position the four cartons on the latter table.

In succession the riders gallop to the changeover line, collect a carton and place it on the table, midway along the arena. The cartons must be stacked on top of each other.

Winning all these rosettes is a pretty tiring business for a young lad

9
ARE YOU A PONY MASTERMIND?

ARE YOU A PONY MASTERMIND?

How much do you really know about ponies? Test yourself, your friends and family with our selection of quizzes. It's a sure way to learn and have fun! You'll find the answers to our brainteasers on pages 118–23.

True or False?

Do you know which of these statements is true and which is incorrect?

1 It's sensible to have your pony vaccinated against tetanus.
2 Ponies can be brought straight out of their stables and galloped in gymkhana practice.
3 In canter there are three beats to every stride.
4 If your pony is healthy, his skin will be supple and loose, and there'll be a bright shine to his coat.
5 When applying a tail bandage you should dampen the tail, not the bandage.
6 If your pony leaves his short feed you should be suspicious.
7 A pony who rushes his jumps enjoys jumping.
8 Ragwort is dangerous only when it is growing.
9 Twisted, Fulmer and German are all types of Pelham bits.
10 A star is a white mark on the forehead.
11 Australian wild horses are called brumbies.
12 It's a good idea to dry tack over a radiator.
13 You should always wash the bit after you've ridden your pony.
14 A pony should jump with a flat back.
15 Dried sugar beet must be soaked before it's fed to ponies and horses.
16 Atherstone, Balding and Lampwick are all types of girth.
17 All thoroughbred horses have the same official birthday of January 1.
18 The best direction for loose boxes to face is north.
19 It's better for stables to have sloping rather than flat roofs.
20 The floor of your pony's stable should have a slight slope from the front to rear of the box.

Thinking Caps On!

Have a go at this set of questions on all aspects of pony care and riding.

1 Ponies need stables which are at least . . . feet by . . . feet.
2 How high and wide should stable doors be?
3 Why should hay racks not be fitted too high above a pony's head?
4 List two advantages of using haynets.
5 What must you remember when tying a hay net?
6 Name three types of straw.
7 Why should you groom your pony?
8 What is a dandy brush used for?
9 When would you use a body brush?
10 How would you use a hoof pick and why?
11 What does quartering mean?
12 If you strap your pony, what are you doing?
13 When is the best time to strap?
14 How much does a horse drink every day?
15 Every day you should swill out and change the water in your pony's water buckets. Why?
16 There's a stream with a sandy bottom in your pony's field. Would you be happy for the pony to drink from the stream?
17 Your pony bolts his feed – how can you slow him down?
18 Name five points to consider when feeding ponies.
19 Name two types of hay.
20 Explain the difference between the two types of hay.
21 Would you buy hay with lots of weeds in it?
22 Why should you ensure when bandaging that the pressure is even all the way along the bandage?
23 Why would you clip your pony?
24 What must you do if you clip a pony?
25 Describe a trace clip.
26 The usual temperature of a pony is . . .
27 At rest a pony's pulse will be between . . . and . . . beats per minute.
28 A pony takes between . . . and . . . breaths a minute at rest.
29 What are the names of the types of teeth a pony has?
30 Name the groove that appears on a pony's teeth around the age of nine or ten.

31 If your pony is said to be rising six what does that mean?
32 You're looking for a pony and the advertisement in your local paper describes one pony as 'aged'. What does that mean?
33 How often does your farrier need to attend to your pony?
34 What's the usual number of nails per shoe?
35 What are the signs that a pony's feet need attention?
36 What is a loriner?
37 Name the measurement used for describing a pony's height.
38 What could cause girth galls?
39 How could you help to prevent girth galls?
40 Your pony has a sore mouth – what could be causing this?
41 What are the natural aids?
42 Whips, spurs and martingales are known as . . . aids.
43 Name an important quality for a gymkhana pony.
44 Where's the final of the Prince Philip Cup?
45 What would it mean if you had to compete *hors concours*?
46 What do the initials MGAGB stand for?
47 The age limit for riders in the Pony Club Mounted Games Championship is . . .
48 In the MGAGB riders can compete up to the age of . . .
49 What year was the PC Mounted Games first introduced to the show that is now its home?
50 If, during a gymkhana game, you make a mistake and do not correct it, what happens?

Twenty-Five Brain Teasers

Test yourself with these quickies.

1 There are . . . beats to every stride in walk.
2 Loose boxes for horses should be . . . feet by . . . feet.
3 Which parts of a pony's body should you avoid using a dandy brush on?
4 When is the best time to give your pony his largest feed?
5 What type of halt should you aim for?
6 New hay is less than . . . months old.
7 The frame upon which a saddle is built is known as the . . .
8 Crushed oats begin to lose their feed value – after how many weeks?
9 Curry combs are used for?
10 How do you know if your stirrup irons are the right size for you?
11 What's the name of the process whereby you put straw under a pony's rug to help him dry off?
12 If you move from halt to trot without walking what type of transition is this known as?
13 As a pony moves along his opposite limbs hit one another, alternately, in the fetlock area. What is this known as?
14 The toe of your pony's hind shoe catches the heel of his foreleg, creating a wound. What's the name of this particular injury?
15 Name the safest type of metal for stirrup irons.
16 How many latches should there be on the bottom stable door?
17 Why would you have sponges in your grooming kit?
18 Name Britain's native breeds of ponies.
19 What's the term for an inexperienced horse or pony?
20 How do you remove a tail bandage?
21 What's the purpose of mane pulling?
22 When's the best time to pull a mane?
23 The mucous membrane of a healthy pony's eye is a particular colour. What is it?
24 If your pony had a temperature of 102°F would you be concerned?
25 What are grass tips?

ANSWERS

True or False Answers

1 True.
2 False – you should always warm up your pony before tackling any type of work. His muscles need to be loosened up – it's not fair on him to ask him to work without any preparation. You wouldn't like to be dragged out of bed and sent on a four-mile run, would you?
3 True.
4 True.
5 True – if you dampen the bandage, once on the tail it may shrink and injure the pony.
6 True – one of the first signs that all is not well with a pony's health is a lack of interest in food. If your pony does not eat up then check for other signs of ill-health, eg high temperature/pulse, increased respiration, uneasy manner. Get to know your pony so that you can instantly recognise any abnormal behaviour and act appropriately.
7 False – a pony usually rushes because he associates jumping with pain or bad memories. Perhaps he is jabbed in the mouth by his rider every time he jumps, or he has a bad back and wants to get the jump and pain over as quickly as possible.
8 False – whether it's dead or alive, ragwort is a highly poisonous plant. If you see any ragwort in your field pull it up by the roots and burn it; otherwise it could kill your pony.
9 False – they are all types of snaffle bits.
10 True – and the mark need not be in the shape of a star.
11 True.
12 False – you'll only succeed in making the leather dry out and crack.
13 True – your pony will appreciate the thought. If you leave the bit dirty it's rather like asking you to eat your meal with dirty cutlery.
14 False – a pony should make a nice rounded shape as he jumps. Ponies who do jump with flat or hollow backs are often experiencing some kind of pain.
15 True – soak sugar beet for at least 12hr. If you feed it without presoaking it can swell up in the pony's stomach and cause serious problems.

16 True.
17 True.
18 False – it's best for loose boxes to face south.
19 True – a sloping roof ensures plenty of air space and light together with natural roof ventilation.
20 True – this allows for drainage.

Thinking Caps On! Answers

1 10ft by 12ft (3 by 3.7m).
2 Stable doors ought to be 8ft (2.4m) high and 4ft (1.2m) wide with the lower part of the door sufficiently high to prevent ponies jumping over.
3 If fitted too high, the pony is forced to feed from an unnatural position, with his head and neck stretched upwards. Also, hay seeds and dust can easily fall into his eyes. It's more natural for a pony to feed from the floor, but the hay can become dirty and soiled.
4 With haynets you can weigh the nets so that you know how much hay your pony is getting. It's also a less wasteful method than feeding from the floor.
5 It's vital that the haynet is tied so that once empty it does not dangle down, creating a hazard. A pony could easily get his leg stuck in a net that was hanging too low.
6 Wheat straw is the best for bedding – there's also oat straw (although this is often eaten by the stable's occupant) and barley straw.
7 Grooming is necessary to promote health, prevent disease, improve appearance and ensure cleanliness. Grooming removes the waste products from your pony's skin, improves his muscle tone and stimulates his circulation.
8 Dandy brushes are used to remove heavily caked mud and dirt from a grasskept pony's coat. The dandy brush should not be used on manes and tails as it tends to split the hairs.
9 Body brushes have smaller, softer bristles than dandy brushes and they remove dust, scurf and grease from the coat. Avoid using a body brush on a pony kept outside, as the pony needs grease in his coat to protect him against the elements. It's fine to use a body brush on the mane and tail.

10 Hoof picks are used to remove mud and stones from the pony's feet. They should be used from heel to toe so that there is no risk of a hoof pick penetrating the soft parts of the frog.

11 Quartering is the name given to the quick brushover given to a pony or horse before it is taken out for exercise. The feet are picked out, the eyes, nose and dock sponged, and the body brushed over quickly.

12 Strapping means giving a pony a thorough grooming – this can take from 30 to 45min if done properly.

13 After exercise – as the pony's pores are then open, and dust and scurf are to the surface.

14 Horses drink between 6 and 10gal (22.5 and 38*l*) of water a day.

15 You should always keep feeding and watering containers scrupulously clean. In addition, standing water absorbs ammonia and other impurities from the air so the water should be changed regularly to ensure that the pony has a good supply of clean, fresh water.

16 If a pony drinks from a sandy bottomed stream he can take in some of the sand particles, which may lead to colic.

17 Adding chaff (chopped hay) to a pony's feed slows him down.

18 Take your pick from these:
    a feed little and often in imitation of the pony's natural method of feeding
    b feed according to work, age, temperament, size
    c feed plenty of bulk (hay) which is required for digestion
    d make no sudden changes in the pony's diet – introduce anything new gradually
    e keep to the same feeding hours daily – ponies like routine and have built in clocks where feeding times are concerned
    f feed only good quality forage
    g feed something succulent each day eg carrots, apples
    h keep feeding utensils clean
    i do not work your pony immediately after feeding – let him have an hour to an hour and a half to digest his feed

19 Seed and meadow hay.

20 Meadow hay is cut from permanent pasture and contains a wide variety of grasses. It's usually soft. Seed hay is cut from land specifically sown for the purpose and the hay is generally hard and of a higher feeding value.

21 No – hay with lots of weeds in shows that the hay has been cut from poor land so there'll be little value in the hay.

22 Uneven pressure, particularly on leg bandages, can result in injuries to the tendons.

23 If your pony was going to be working hard through the winter he would be less likely to sweat and lose condition if he was clipped. It's easier to dry a clipped pony and to keep him clean.

24 By clipping you are removing all or some of the pony's thick winter coat, so you'll have to replace it with an artificial means of keeping warm, ie rugs and underblankets as required.

25 For a trace clip, the hair is removed from the pony's belly, the top of his legs and underneath his neck.

26 100–101°F.

27 36–42.

28 8–15.

29 Molars are the grinding teeth while incisors are the biting teeth. Males also usually have two tushes in each jaw. Wolf teeth are only small, with tiny roots and are often removed as they serve no purpose.

30 Galvayne's groove.

31 The pony is almost six years of age.

32 The pony is more than eight years of age.

33 A pony's feet need attention every four to six weeks.

34 Four on the outside and three on the inside, but the fewer nails the better. The healthier the foot, the fewer nails are needed to hold the shoe in place.

35 The pony may have cast or lost a shoe, the shoe could be worn thin or be loose. Clenches may have risen. The pony's foot may be long and out of shape.

36 A maker of bits.

37 Hands – each hand is equivalent to 4in (101.6mm).

38 Girths that are hard because they have not been properly cleaned or looked after; girths that are too tight or too loose can rub and cause galls.

39 Galls can be prevented by taking proper care of tack; ensuring that the girth is sufficiently tight but not too tight; pulling the pony's forelegs forwards to remove any crinkles in the skin once the girth has been adjusted; using saline solution or witch-hazel to harden the skin of a pony in soft condition.

40 A bit injury – if the bit is rough or of the wrong size. Rough handed riders can also injure their ponies.
41 The rider's seat, legs, hands, weight, thought, voice.
42 Artificial aids.
43 Gymkhana ponies must be forward-going, balanced and supple.
44 At the Horse of the Year Show.
45 You'd be riding non-competitively, ie your score would not count.
46 Mounted Games Association of Great Britain.
47 Under 15 years of age on May 1.
48 21 – riders must be under 21 on January 1 to be eligible.
49 1957
50 You are eliminated.

Twenty-Five Brain Teasers Answers

1 Four.
2 Twelve feet by fourteen feet.
3 Head, mane and tail.
4 In the evening – he then has lots of time to digest it.
5 A square halt.
6 Six.
7 Tree.
8 Three.
9 Cleaning the body brush. Rubber curry combs can also be used in a circular manner to remove caked mud and dirt, but should not be used on bony parts, eg the pony's head.
10 With the broadest part of your foot in the stirrup there should be ½in (12mm) clearance at either side. If the iron is too big there's the danger of the foot slipping through, whereas if the iron is too small the rider's foot could become jammed.
11 Thatching.
12 Acute transition.
13 Brushing.
14 An overreach.
15 Stainless steel.
16 Two – one bolt at the top plus another at the bottom. Some ponies are adept at undoing bolts and a bottom bolt prevents these would-be Houdinis from escaping. For ease, the bottom bolt can be foot-operated.

17 You'd use separate sponges for cleaning the eyes, nose and dock.
18 Dartmoor; Exmoor; Fell; Dales; Shetland; Connemara; Welsh; Highland and New Forest.
19 A 'green' pony.
20 Get hold of the bandage at the root of the tail and slide it downwards and off.
21 To thin out a thick mane, shorten the mane and help it to lie flat.
22 After exercise as the pony's pores are open.
23 Salmon pink.
24 YES! This is a high temperature.
25 Grass tips are thin, half length shoes used on ponies out at grass to stop the wall in the toe region from splitting.

APPENDIX

SPECIAL INFORMATION FOR OWNERS AND RIDERS
OF SHETLAND PONIES

Gymkhana events feature strongly in the Shetland Pony Stud Book
Society with a Performance Award Scheme, based on a points system.

In order to qualify for the scheme the Shetlands must be
registered with the society. The scheme works in the following way:
points are gained from either winning or being placed in a variety of
equestrian activities, including mounted games, at shows which are
affiliated to the Shetland Pony Stud Book Society; the British Horse
Society; National Show Pony Society; Ponies of Britain and British
Driving Society.

Performance awards are presented annually to the competitors
gaining the most points – the most sought-after award is, of course,
the championship.

The society was formed in 1980 by Pat Leivers of Leicestershire
who's a Shetland pony lover and recognised the versatility of the
breed. 'I introduced the scheme in an effort to encourage people to
ride and use Shetlands for they are good, all-round ponies and make
excellent mounts for children,' explained Pat.

'The scheme got off the ground with a ridden section with three
classes which covered lead rein, off the lead rein and gymkhanas.
The interest increased to such an extent that we expanded into
working pony classes, handy pony, mountain and moorland classes,
as well as Riding For The Disabled events.

'In fact, the scheme has snowballed – it's both remarkable and
encouraging to see how many Shetland ponies are used over the
country as a whole.'

Having spent eight years nurturing the scheme and watching it
grow from humble beginnings, Pat has now handed over the reins to
colleague Vivienne Hampton. 'I fulfilled my ambition, to introduce
the scheme, get it off the ground and watch it grow,' said Pat. 'Now I
want to take a back seat – although I am still involved, it is more in an

advisory capacity so that I am free to get on with other things.'

But there is still a great deal that Pat is involved in – for instance she still runs the administration of the scheme as well as the Shetland displays at fun days.

In 1987 there was a Riding For The Disabled Shetland fun event at Gatcombe Park where eight Shetlands and their riders competed against eight celebrities in a gymkhana event.

'I thoroughly enjoy organising the fun events,' said Pat, who clearly has no intention of giving up assisting the society. 'I thoroughly enjoy Shetland ponies and the work the society is involved in.'

Anyone interested in joining the Shetland Pony Stud Book Society Performance Award Scheme should contact Mrs Vivienne Hampton at Larkins, High Elms Lane, Benington, Nr Stevenage, Herts.

INDEX